"[The authors] have provided patients with an essential map and guidebook for people with bipolar II disorder who, by no fault of their own, have become strangers in a strange land. This book includes essential tools that can help people manage their disorder and find their way to wellness and functioning."

—**Andrew A. Nierenberg, MD**, professor of psychiatry at Harvard Medical School, director at the Bipolar Clinic and Research Program at Massachusetts General Hospital, and associate director of the Depression Clinical and Research Program at Massachusetts General Hospital

"Bipolar II is a lifelong and often difficult challenge for those who have the disorder and those who care for them. But *The Bipolar II Disorder Workbook* will help you cope by teaching you how to notice your mood changes, how to turn around your depression or hypomania, and how to help others understand what you are going through. This workbook will give you the tools to work on [managing] your disorder. Written in a clear, easily accessible style, with lots of self-help forms and techniques, this book will be of use whenever things get too high or too low. I highly recommend this very useful guide."

—**Robert L. Leahy, PhD**, director at the American Institute for Cognitive Therapy, associate editor at the *International Journal of Cognitive Therapy*, and clinical professor of psychology at Weill-Cornell University Medical College, New York Presbyterian Hospital

"With refreshingly clear language, three experts in the field draw from the best science in the area to provide a clear road map for how to come to terms with bipolar II disorder. This book offers great advice on how to recognize and gain better control over manic, depressive, and anxious symptoms."

—**Sheri L. Johnson, PhD**, director at Cal Mania (Calm) and lab professor of psychology at the University of California, Berkeley

"This workbook is grounded in cutting-edge research for treating mood and anxiety disorders, but distills this broad literature into a user-friendly set of skills specific to managing bipolar disorder, type II. Roberts, Sylvia, and Reilly-Harrington give readers tools that they can apply to their own lives to feel better, such as education about bipolar II and ways to manage negative thinking, temper anxiety, gain social support, and develop a comprehensive wellness plan. This book is a must-read for anyone whose experience of mood disturbance is an obstacle to leading a fuller life."

—**Lauren B. Alloy, PhD**, professor, Joseph Wolpe Distinguished Faculty Fellow, and director of clinical training at Temple University, Philadelphia, PA

"I highly recommend this book. The authors—leading researchers in this field—have provided a great service to individuals suffering from bipolar II disorder, their families, and mental health care professionals. Useful as a guide and workbook, this book can be used by individuals seeking to learn about the disorder individually, or as a tool in therapy. This concise and very approachable book condenses the latest research on the treatments for bipolar II disorder, helps readers to understand what is unique about this disorder, and reviews the best treatments available. There are excellent chapters on the management of depression, mania, and anxiety that are filled with good advice and practical, problem-solving techniques that will immediately be helpful."

> —**Edward S. Friedman, MD**, associate professor of psychiatry at the University of Pittsburgh; director of the Mood Disorders Treatment and Research Program at the University of Pittsburgh; and director of cognitive behavior therapy and adult ambulatory pharmacotherapy training programs at Western Psychiatric Institute and Clinic, Pittsburgh, PA

"What a great book! By combining education, tools for self-monitoring, and step-by-step treatments, the authors have created a resource for patients and families with bipolar II disorder that will be used again and again. Roberts, Sylvia, and Reilly-Harrington are skilled therapists, and this workbook is like having access to them any hour of the day."

> —**Michael J. Ostacher, MD, MPH, MMSc**, assistant professor of psychiatry in the department of psychiatry and behavioral sciences at Stanford University School of Medicine, CA, and associate director of the bipolar disorder and depression research program at the Veterans Affairs Palo Alto Health Care System in Palo Alto, CA, where he is also director of the Mental Illness Research Education and Clinical Center (MIRECC) fellowship program

"This is a great resource for the many patients and professionals who seek better ways to manage bipolar disorder but don't want to reinvent the wheel or waste time searching for tools. We owe the authors our thanks for assembling a treasure trove of excellent tools and the instructions necessary to put them to effective use."

> —**Gary Sachs, MD**, associate clinical professor of psychiatry at Harvard Medical School in Boston, MA

THE
Bipolar II
DISORDER
WORKBOOK

Managing Recurring Depression, Hypomania & Anxiety

STEPHANIE McMURRICH ROBERTS, PhD
LOUISA GRANDIN SYLVIA, PhD
NOREEN A. REILLY-HARRINGTON, PhD

New Harbinger Publications, Inc.

Publisher's Note

This publication is designed to provide accurate and authoritative information in regard to the subject matter covered. It is sold with the understanding that the publisher is not engaged in rendering psychological, financial, legal, or other professional services. If expert assistance or counseling is needed, the services of a competent professional should be sought.

Distributed in Canada by Raincoast Books

Copyright © 2013 by Stephanie McMurrich Roberts, Louisa Sylvia, and
Noreen Reilly-Harrington
New Harbinger Publications, Inc.
5674 Shattuck Avenue
Oakland, CA 94609
www.newharbinger.com

Cover design by Sara Christian; Text design by Tracy Marie Carlson;
Acquired by Catharine Meyers; Edited by Will DeRooy

Library of Congress Cataloging-in-Publication Data on file

Printed in the United States of America

23   22   21

15   14   13   12

To all of our clients, for teaching us so much and allowing us to be a part of your lives. This book would not have been possible without you.

—S.M.R.

—L.G.S.

—N.R.H.

Contents

PART 4
How to Manage Anxiety

PART 5
Finding Support and Creating a Personalized Wellness Plan

Foreword

Bipolar II disorder is a highly misunderstood form of bipolar illness. By its very designation as type II, clinicians, patients, and the public often assume it is less impairing than bipolar I, "the real thing." When we examine the diagnostic criteria for bipolar II, they sound very mild. Who doesn't get sad and happy? Who doesn't have mood swings? Why would a four-day period of excess energy, which does not affect the ability to function, be of any clinical importance?

Several longitudinal studies have found that bipolar II is far more impairing than we once thought. It is characterized by lengthy and recurrent periods of depression, comorbid anxiety disorders, and high rates of substance and alcohol misuse. The occasional hypomanias of bipolar II—in which people experience elation and irritability, exuberance, increased energy, and reduced need to sleep—are not as impairing as the full manic episodes of bipolar I, but they can certainly have a negative impact on family members and friends. Moreover, for the person with the disorder, these high periods are often short-lived, and they do little to alleviate the suffering caused by depressive phases. The hypomanic periods may even overlap with the low phases, resulting in an agitated, anxiety-ridden, and highly distressing period of depression. People with bipolar II often have difficulty maintaining jobs and relationships, and, like people with bipolar I, they are at high risk for suicide.

The self-management tools that have been developed for bipolar disorder—such as identifying early warning signs of mania and trying to prevent further escalation—are primarily meant for people with bipolar I disorder who have full remissions between episodes. One can find many self-help books that explain these strategies, but few address the needs that are specific to the bipolar II syndrome. This book fills this gap. The authors, Stephanie Roberts, PhD, Louisa Sylvia, PhD, and Noreen Reilly-Harrington, PhD, are highly experienced clinicians and researchers who have years of experience working with people with bipolar disorder. In this workbook, they present strategies for managing the depressive and hypomanic phases unique to bipolar II disorder. Some of these strategies, such as the use of thought restructuring and behavioral activation, may already be familiar to readers from the depression literature. However, the book expands upon these cognitive behavioral strategies and introduces novel approaches, such as the use of mindfulness and lifestyle management skills for mood episodes. Furthermore, this book provides self-care tools for anxiety, a common co-occurring condition for people with bipolar II disorder. By the end of this book, readers will have learned skills to create a personalized wellness plan that outlines strategies for staying healthy. The plan strongly encourages the involvement of family members and other support systems.

Readers with bipolar II disorder and their family members will find this book useful in furthering their knowledge of this disease. Most of all, they will come away with a sense of hope that it can be managed with more than just medications. We have a long way to go before we fully understand the care of bipolar disorder and its variants. In this highly readable book, these authors have helped move us forward in caring for people with bipolar II disorder.

—David J. Miklowitz, PhD
    Co-founder, family-focused treatment (FFT)
    Los Angeles, California

Introduction

This workbook provides helpful, easy-to-understand information about bipolar II disorder (BPII) and what differentiates it from bipolar I disorder (BPI), as well as strategies for managing it. The exercises in this book are geared toward individuals who have been diagnosed with BPII; however, family members and friends of people with BPII, as well as clinicians and educators, will no doubt find this book a valuable source of information about BPII and its management.

The Purpose of This Book

Before we get started, it is important to acknowledge that BPII is a complex, chronic mental illness, and there is no simple way to manage it. The first line of treatment for BPII is almost always psychiatric medication; however, beyond medication, there are many strategies for minimizing symptoms, reducing relapse, and maximizing well-being. This book is designed to introduce you to a range of strategies so that you can build a collection of tools for managing your BPII. The primary goal of this book is to help you feel more in control of your BPII, or become "a better captain of your own ship." We don't expect that every single tool will be helpful to you, but our hope is that you will find many of them useful.

How This Book Is Different

This book is different from similar workbooks because of its focus on BPII, which is treated and managed differently than BPI. This book also includes strategies for managing anxiety, which frequently co-occurs with BPII. Finally, as opposed to other books, in this book we present strategies from several different psychotherapeutic approaches, such as cognitive behavioral therapy

(CBT), family-focused treatment (FFT), and dialectical behavior therapy (DBT). Although some of these skills were developed from research studies involving people without bipolar disorder, we will show you how they can be applied to the specific needs of people with BPII.

How to Use This Book

After defining BPII in chapter 1, we will give an overview of the different psychotherapeutic approaches in chapter 2 and then explore the skills of these therapies in more depth in the chapters that follow. The final two chapters will discuss how to build a support team of family, friends, and professional care providers who can help you better manage your illness.

Pace Yourself

Each chapter focuses on a different topic or strategy, and many chapters have exercises for you to complete. If you read the book quickly, you will likely feel overwhelmed by all the information. Thus, we recommend that you read only one chapter every one to two weeks. This way you can think carefully about the concepts and have enough time to practice the skills before moving on to a new chapter and set of skills. In between reading the chapters, you should focus on practicing the skills on a daily basis, because learning a new skill always requires practice! You will undoubtedly get the most out of this book if you allow yourself to learn one new skill at a time in each chapter.

Use the Accompanying Website

Many of the exercises in this book can be found at http://www.newharbinger.com/27664 (see the back of this book for more information) so that you can download and print copies of the ones that you find most useful. You can also download audio files for the mindfulness and relaxation techniques you will learn in chapters 6 and 10.

Use This Book Alone or with a Therapist

This book was written so that you could learn to apply the tools for managing BPII independently. However, if you are currently working with a therapist, you may find it helpful to work through the book together.

This book is not intended to be used in place of professional help. If you have not received a diagnosis of BPII, but think that you may have it or another psychiatric condition, you should contact a health care professional as soon as possible.

Be Hopeful

There is no doubt that living with and managing the symptoms of BPII can be difficult. There are probably times when you feel helpless and overwhelmed. The tools in this book are designed to help you handle your mood swings and to feel more confident in your ability to do so. Our hope and intent for you is that, after implementing the skills taught in this book, you begin to feel that *you* are in control of your disorder, rather than the disorder being in control of you. So keep an open mind and a hopeful attitude—you have more power over your illness than you may think!

PART 1

Understanding Bipolar Disorder

CHAPTER 1

What Is Bipolar II Disorder?

In this chapter, we explain how a diagnosis of bipolar II disorder (BPII) is made (APA 2013). BPII differs from the other main type of bipolar disorder, bipolar I (BPI), in two key ways. First, everyone with BPII experiences one or more periods of depression; however, depression may or may not be present in BPI. Second, people with BPII experience *hypomania*, a less severe version of *mania*, the episodic high or elevated mood that is the defining feature of BPI.

Let's look more closely at both BPI and BPII.

Bipolar Disorder, Type I

When people talk about "bipolar disorder" they are often referring to BPI, which is quite different from BPII. Individuals with BPI experience *manic episodes* (table 1.1). Manic episodes are characterized by either elevated mood or extreme irritability (e.g., abnormally high or oddly cheerful mood), accompanied by at least three of the other manic symptoms listed in table 1.1, over most of the day for *at least* seven days (APA 2013).

Table 1.1. Diagnostic Criteria of Types of Bipolar Mood Episodes

Episode	Minimum Duration	Symptoms	Impairment*
Depressive	2 weeks	Depressed mood or loss of interest or pleasure plus FOUR or more of the following: • Weight loss or weight gain • Insomnia/hypersomnia • Restlessness/agitation or feeling very slowed down • Fatigue/loss of energy • Feelings of worthlessness or guilt • Trouble concentrating/making decisions • Thoughts of death/suicidal ideation	Yes
Manic	1 week	Elevated mood or irritability plus THREE** or more of the following: • Abnormally high self-esteem • A decreased need for sleep • Feeling more talkative than usual or a pressure to keep talking • Racing thoughts or more ideas than usual • Distractibility • An increase in goal-directed behavior • Involvement in pleasurable activities that have a high likelihood to have negative consequences	Yes
Hypomanic	4 days	Elevated mood or irritability plus THREE** or more of the following: • Abnormally high self-esteem • A decreased need for sleep • Feeling more talkative than usual or a pressure to keep talking • Racing thoughts or more ideas than usual • Distractibility • An increase in goal-directed behavior • Involvement in pleasurable activities that have a high likelihood to have negative consequences	No

* Impairment means that the symptoms cause significant distress or difficulty functioning in some important way (e.g., you are not able to work, it causes problems with your family or friends).

** Four of these symptoms are required if you are experiencing predominantly irritable (as opposed to elevated) mood.

You may have heard people say that they feel "manic" on days when they have high energy or are in a particularly cheerful mood, perhaps even experiencing some of the manic symptoms listed in table 1.1, but this is not necessarily mania. For example, over the holidays, people may report feeling very happy and excited, have increased energy, sleep less than usual, and talk more than usual. If these "symptoms" last more than seven days, are these people actually experiencing mania? Certainly not! So, what is the difference between periods of good mood, or high energy, and mania?

The difference is that when you are experiencing mania, your symptoms make it difficult for you to fulfill your responsibilities with regard to work, to friends and family, or to yourself (self-care). In other words, the symptoms associated with a manic episode interfere with your ability to function (e.g., to work, to pay bills, to take care of children, to see your friends, to accomplish daily tasks), which causes problems for you (e.g., you show up late for work, you're not able to pay bills, your relationships with friends and family suffer, you can't accomplish daily tasks). This *impairment* is a required part of a BPI diagnosis (table 1.2).

You can see in table 1.2 that the main criterion for a BPI diagnosis is a manic episode (either by itself or as part of a mixed episode—a manic and depressive episode *at the same time*). Neither hypomania nor depression (either by itself or as part of a mixed episode) is *required* for a BPI diagnosis, yet both are required for a diagnosis of BPII.

Table 1.2. Different Types of Bipolar Disorder

Bipolar Disorder	Manic Episode	Hypomanic Episode	Depressive Episode	Mixed Episode*
Type I	Yes	Possibly	Possibly	Possibly
Type II	No	Yes	Yes	Possibly

Note. "Yes" means that such an episode is required for the diagnosis. "No" means that such an episode indicates a different diagnosis. "Possibly" means that such an episode can occur with this diagnosis, but it is not required for the diagnosis.

* Mixed episodes are manic or hypomanic episodes with three depressive symptoms occuring at the same time or a depressive episode with at least three manic/hypomanic symptoms occuring at the same time.

Bipolar II Disorder

BPII is the focus of this book; a set of questions at the end of this chapter will help you determine whether you have BPII. As mentioned, a BPII diagnosis includes depression and hypomania (see table 1.2).

Depression

A major depressive episode, often called "depression" or "clinical depression," means that you have felt down or sad, or much less interested in things than usual, for most of the day, nearly every day, for at least two weeks. In addition to feeling sad or less interested in things, you have at least *four* other depressive symptoms (see table 1.1).

On a "bad day," many people may say that they are depressed. They may also describe symptoms of depression, such as feeling tired, having trouble sleeping, or having negative thoughts about themselves (e.g., *I am lazy*; *I am not attractive*). This does not mean they are actually experiencing a depressive episode. These types of "bad days" do not tend to last for at least two weeks and are not associated with at least five of the depressive symptoms listed in table 1.1 during the same two-week period. Most importantly, many people have bad days, but the symptoms they experience on those days typically do not interfere with their ability to function (e.g., to work, to take care of children) and do not lead to *impairment* (i.e., inability to accomplish daily tasks). As with mania, impairment *must* accompany the sad mood or loss of interest (as well as the other symptoms listed in table 1.1) in order for this to be considered a depressive episode.

Hypomania

Hypomania is characterized by a persistently irritable, elevated, or expansive mood, accompanied by at least three of the other hypomanic symptoms (or four with irritable mood) listed in table 1.1, over most of the day for *at least* four days. You may notice that the symptoms listed for hypomania and mania in table 1.1 are the same. Hypomania differs from mania in that such an episode is typically shorter and is less severe, given that it does not impair functioning. Once the symptoms impair functioning, the episode is almost always considered a manic episode, unless it is only brief (e.g., less than seven days).

Given that people may report feeling "manic" during the holidays, you can imagine how hypomania may be confused even more frequently with normal mood given that it does not require impairment. A few tips to help you further distinguish hypomania is to remember that hypomania is *abnormally* high or irritable mood, meaning different from what a person usually experiences when happy or upset/irritable. Hypomanic episodes also last for at least four consecutive days. Thus, this *abnormally* high or irritable mood persists for several days and is accompanied by at least three (or four, if the mood is irritable) of the manic/hypomanic symptoms in table 1.1 *for the same four days*. Finally, in order to be diagnosed with BPII, you must have also experienced a major depressive episode at some time in your life.

Table 1.3. Summary of Differences Between Bipolar Diagnoses

Criteria for Diagnosis	BPI	BPII
Type of episode(s)	Mania (and possibly depression)	Hypomania and Depression
Duration for mood elevation	At least 7 days	At least 4 days
Duration for depression	If present, 14 days	14 days
Impairment	Yes	Yes (during depressive episodes only)

Note. BPI = Bipolar I disorder, BPII = Bipolar II disorder.

To help you understand what type of bipolar disorder you may have, complete the following exercise.

Exercise 1.1.
Self-Test: Goldberg Bipolar Screening Inventory

Circle the response that best indicates how much you agree with each of the following statements, in a way that reflects how you have felt and behaved over much of your life. If you have usually been one way, and have recently changed, your responses should reflect how you have usually been. (In order for the results of this quiz to be most accurate, you should be eighteen or older and have had at least one episode of depression.) When you have finished, use the key at the bottom of the test to score your answers.

Statement	Agree	Score
At times, I am much more talkative or speak much faster than usual.	• Not at all • Just a little • Somewhat • Moderately • Quite a lot • Very much	

Statement	Agree	Score
There have been times when I was much more active or did many more things than usual.	• Not at all • Just a little • Somewhat • Moderately • Quite a lot • Very much	
I get into moods where I feel very "sped-up" or irritable.	• Not at all • Just a little • Somewhat • Moderately • Quite a lot • Very much	
There have been times when I have felt both high (elated) and low (depressed) at the same time.	• Not at all • Just a little • Somewhat • Moderately • Quite a lot • Very much	
I have been much more interested in sex than usual.	• Not at all • Just a little • Somewhat • Moderately • Quite a lot • Very much	
My self-confidence ranges from great self-doubt to equally great overconfidence.	• Not at all • Just a little • Somewhat • Moderately • Quite a lot • Very much	
There have been great variations in the quantity or quality of my work.	• Not at all • Just a little • Somewhat • Moderately • Quite a lot • Very much	

		TOTAL SCORE:
For no apparent reason I sometimes have been very angry or hostile.	• Not at all • Just a little • Somewhat • Moderately • Quite a lot • Very much	
I have periods of mental dullness and other periods of very creative thinking.	• Not at all • Just a little • Somewhat • Moderately • Quite a lot • Very much	
At times I am greatly interested in being with people and at other times I just want to be left alone with my thoughts.	• Not at all • Just a little • Somewhat • Moderately • Quite a lot • Very much	
I have had periods of great optimism and other periods of equally great pessimism.	• Not at all • Just a little • Somewhat • Moderately • Quite a lot • Very much	
I have had periods of tearfulness and crying and other times when I laugh and joke excessively.	• Not at all • Just a little • Somewhat • Moderately • Quite a lot • Very much	
Scoring: For each answer, give the following score on that item: Not at all = 0 Moderately = 3 Just a little = 1 Quite a lot = 4 Somewhat = 2 Very much = 5		TOTAL SCORE:

Understanding Your Score

If your total score is *lower than 9*, you likely do not have any mood disorder. Thus, your experiences fall in a normal range and do not suggest that you have concerning symptoms. If your score is *between 9 and 15*, you are experiencing normal mood fluctuations, or perhaps some depression, but your symptoms still do not suggest a bipolar diagnosis. If your score is *between 16 and 24*, you may be experiencing some depression and possibly hypomania, or BPII. If you scored *higher than 25*, you are experiencing enough symptoms at a high enough intensity to suggest a bipolar diagnosis, either BPI or BPII. A score *higher than 36* indicates moderate to severe symptoms of bipolar disorder and thus suggests a BPI diagnosis. Remember that these ranges are estimates and *this test is not a diagnostic tool.* If you think you qualify for either type of bipolar disorder, we strongly recommend that you speak with a doctor. The information provided in this chapter is not intended as a substitute for an evaluation with a professional care provider.

Chapter Summary:

- Mania is the defining feature of BPI.

- Depression and hypomania are the defining features of BPII.

- Impairment from depressive symptoms, but not hypomanic symptoms, is necessary to be diagnosed with BPII.

- Consult a doctor if you are unsure whether your symptoms meet criteria for bipolar disorder.

CHAPTER 2

Understanding the Treatments for Bipolar II Disorder and a Guide to Using This Book

Treatment for bipolar II disorder (BPII) typically consists of both medication and therapy. In this chapter, we review the medications and psychosocial therapies commonly used to treat BPII. We also lay out which chapters discuss which skills for managing BPII, to help you use this book more effectively.

Common Medications for BPII

BPII is considered a *biological illness* because it is associated with structural and functional abnormalities in the brain. In recent years, psychologists have learned much about how the brain of someone with BPII differs from that of someone without the disorder; however, because the brain is very complex, there is still a lot that we do not understand. We know that BPII is caused, at least in part, by problems with the brain's chemical messengers, or *neurotransmitters*. But it seems that each person with BPII may have slightly different problems with his or her neurotransmitters and we don't yet understand exactly what these differences are. Thus, it is not unusual for doctors to be unsure of the best approach to treat a person's particular symptoms. As a result, there is usually some trial and error involved in prescribing medication for BPII. The good news is that there are many medications that can be helpful, and every year health care professionals become more knowledgeable about how to treat BPII with these medications. The other piece of good news is that when used in combination with therapy, or in conjunction with many of the skills taught in this book, medication can decrease the likelihood of mood episodes.

Let us give a brief overview of the key classes of medication used to treat BPII.

Mood Stabilizers (Lithium and Anticonvulsants)

Mood stabilizers are psychiatric medications used to treat mood disorders characterized by intense and sustained mood shifts, such as bipolar disorder. This class of medication is typically the first line of treatment for bipolar disorder because it is particularly helpful in controlling hypomanic and manic symptoms.

Lithium is the oldest medication used to treat bipolar disorder, having been approved by the US Food and Drug Administration in the 1970s. It is also particularly effective in managing both mania and depression. All medications have side effects, but lithium can be particularly toxic. Therefore, if you take this medication your doctor will ask that you have regular blood tests to check the amount of lithium in your blood. Doctors are becoming very practiced at prescribing lithium, and it remains a popular drug to try first in treating bipolar disorder.

Lithium is the only mood stabilizer not also considered to be an anticonvulsant. Although anticonvulsants were originally designed to treat seizures, it was discovered that they also help control mood. They are also used to prevent migraines and treat epilepsy and other brain disorders. When they were first used for treating bipolar disorder, anticonvulsants were prescribed for people who did not respond to lithium, but now they are often prescribed alone, with lithium, or with an antipsychotic (see below). Anticonvulsants include valproic acid (Depakote), lamotrigine (Lamictal), gabapentin (Neurontin), topiramate (Topamax), and oxcarbazepine (Trileptal).

Antidepressants

Examples of antidepressants are fluoxetine (Prozac), paroxetine (Paxil), sertraline (Zoloft), and bupropion (Wellbutrin). Given that people with BPII are more prone to depression than to hypomania (see chapter 1), it is common for individuals with BPII to be treated with both an antidepressant and a mood stabilizer. However, a recent, large study found that taking an antidepressant in combination with a mood stabilizer is *not* a more effective treatment for depression than taking a mood stabilizer alone (Sachs et al. 2007). This suggests that a mood stabilizer alone is likely the best treatment for BPII. Nevertheless, as mentioned, each person may require a slightly different regimen of medication, so it is always best to speak with your doctor to determine what medication or medications may be most effective for you.

Atypical Antipsychotics

The atypical antipsychotics are olanzapine (Zyprexa), aripiprazole (Abilify), quetiapine (Seroquel), risperidone (Risperdal), ziprasidone (Geodon), and asenapine (Saphris). They are called "atypical" to differentiate them from earlier antipsychotics (e.g., Haldol) produced in the 1950s and 1960s.

As you might guess, these medications are mostly used to manage psychotic symptoms (e.g., seeing or hearing things that others do not see or hear, having false or unusual beliefs), but they can also be very effective in managing hypomania and mania. They are best used to treat acute mania, and therefore they are more often prescribed for individuals with BPI than for those with BPII. Quetiapine is the only atypical antipsychotic currently approved by the US Food and Drug Administration for the treatment of bipolar disorder; however, doctors can still prescribe any of the others to someone with bipolar disorder if they believe it would be helpful for particular symptoms (this is called *off-label use*).

The preceding brief overview of the medications used to treat bipolar disorder is certainly not an exhaustive list. For example, Symbyax, approved by the US Food and Drug Administration for the treatment of bipolar disorder, is a medication that combines an antidepressant (fluoxetine) with an antipsychotic (olanzapine). *Benzodiazepines* (e.g., Ativan, Valium, Klonopin, Xanax) may be used to treat anxiety, which commonly co-occurs with bipolar disorder. In addition, many different types of medications may be used to treat the side effects of medications or other co-occurring disorders.

Why Use a Skills-Based Therapy?

As we just discussed, BPII is related to chemicals in your brain, but BPII is also very much influenced by your environment and how you choose to respond to situations and events.

Imagine your favorite major league baseball player. He is likely fast and strong, and has excellent vision. However, stress in his environment could affect his ability to run, throw, catch, or hit. For example, if it was the bottom of the ninth inning and the score was tied, might this stressful situation affect his thoughts, feelings, and behaviors? Could it make it harder for him to hit the ball or run the bases? Or does he do well under pressure, often rising to the occasion and hitting better during stressful situations?

We use this example to demonstrate how people may be affected by their biology (e.g., innate strength and speed) as well as by their environment (e.g., stress or high-pressure situations). When we apply this phenomenon to explaining BPII, it is called the diathesis-stress model. The diathesis-stress model suggests that diseased conditions, such as BPII, are affected by both people's genes (i.e., biological causes) and their environment (Ingram and Luxton 2005). Another way to think about this phenomenon is to picture two people who are stuck in traffic and are late for a meeting; one of these individuals has BPII and the other does not. The diathesis-stress model suggests that the individual with BPII is more likely to be negatively affected by this stressful situation than the person without BPII. In other words, due to his or her biology, the person with BPII may have a lower threshold for tolerating negative events. For example, an individual with BPII is more likely to have negative thoughts when stuck in traffic, such as *My friend is going to be so mad at me because I will be late*, and act in potentially unhealthy ways, such as driving recklessly or canceling the meeting, and thus feel more negatively (e.g., sad, angry, disappointed). In short, the biological tendencies of the individual with BPII are interacting with the situation to create a more negative outcome.

The good news is that skills-based therapies can help you control your responses to the stress in your environment by helping you manage your thoughts, feelings, and behaviors. In other words, using these skills can make situations seem less stressful. Furthermore, it means that skills-based therapy, or learning ways to respond to your environment more thoughtfully, can help you manage episodes of depression and hypomania. In fact, the skills-based therapies that we discuss in this book have been found to be *just as effective as medication* in managing BPII (Lam et al. 2005).

Skills-Based Therapies for BPII

In the past fifteen years, clinicians have learned a lot about BPII and how to treat it. As a result, several new therapeutic strategies have been developed to help manage mood symptoms and increase periods of wellness for people with BPII (table 2.1). In this section we describe each of these treatments as well as the research that supports their effectiveness.

Table 2.1. Summary of Psychotherapies Used to Treat Bipolar II Disorder

Therapy	Developer (Year)	Major Theme
Cognitive behavioral therapy (CBT)	Aaron Beck et al. (1979)	Changing dysfunctional thoughts and behaviors
Dialectical behavior therapy (DBT)	Marsha Linehan (1993)	Increasing awareness of thoughts, feelings, and behaviors and observing them nonjudgmentally
Mindfulness-based cognitive therapy (MBCT)	Zindel Segal, Mark Williams, and John Teasdale (2002)	Learning to pay attention in a particular way, on purpose, in the present moment
Family-focused treatment (FFT)	David Miklowitz and Michael Goldstein (1997)	Reducing stress and improving communication in the home environment
Interpersonal and social rhythm therapy (IPSRT)	Ellen Frank (2005)	Stabilizing daily routine, managing symptoms, and resolving interpersonal problems
Psychoeducation (PE)	Francesc Colom and Eduard Vieta (2006)	Emphasizes psycho-bio-social model, core psychosocial issues, and user-friendly format

Cognitive Behavioral Therapy

One of the most well-known psychotherapies is cognitive behavioral therapy (CBT), which combines cognitive therapy and behavioral therapy. Cognitive therapy, developed by Dr. Aaron Beck and his colleagues in the 1970s, focuses on how to change unrealistic, unhelpful thoughts into more realistic, helpful, and accurate ones. Behavioral therapy is designed to change unhelpful behaviors; it is based on learning theory, which emerged from the work of Drs. Ivan Pavlov, John Watson, and Clark Hull in the early 20th century. Learning theory helped show how people might be able to train themselves to do new behaviors—for example, chewing gum instead of smoking. Changing your behaviors requires practice; it also requires that you make big changes one small step at a time, with these steps often facilitated by rewards for previous ones. This book will give you skills to teach yourself new, healthier behaviors around everyday habits like eating and sleeping.

In the 1980s, doctors and researchers realized that it was essential to merge cognitive and behavioral therapy because thoughts and behavior clearly influenced each other. Imagine a day when you wake up thinking that you do not want to go to work—perhaps there is a meeting that you do not want to go to. This thought will make it much more difficult for you to get up and go to work. In this way, your *thoughts* impact how you behave, or what you *do*. However, what you *do* also influences your *thoughts*. Have you ever noticed that it is easier to think about going to work after you have showered or gotten dressed? The act of showering and dressing, or doing these things, may help you think more positively about going to work. In short, your behaviors influence your thinking and vice versa.

Merging cognitive therapy and behavioral therapy also made sense because both your thoughts and behaviors influence your mood. This is particularly important because it is very difficult to change your mood without first changing your thinking or behaviors. In other words, people typically have trouble spontaneously changing their mood. Can you just suddenly feel happy, like turning on a switch? Try it right now, before you read further.

If you were successful at changing your mood, we are willing to bet that you either had to think about something first (i.e., cognitive therapy) or do something (i.e., behavioral therapy). Perhaps you thought of a happy childhood memory or poured yourself a cup of coffee, which may have evoked positive feelings. On the contrary, perhaps you remembered a conflict with a friend or stubbed your toe, which may have triggered negative feelings.

Several researchers have found that CBT, a therapy focused on changing people's thoughts *and* behaviors to help them feel better, enables individuals with bipolar disorder to manage their mood (Ball et al. 2006; Cochran 1984; Perry et al. 1999; Scott 2001; Zaretsky, Segal, and Gemar 1999). One study of over 100 people with bipolar disorder found that those who received CBT had fewer and shorter mood episodes (hypomania or depression) and fewer hospital admissions compared to those who did not receive CBT (Lam et al. 1999). Those who received CBT also exhibited better social functioning, and reported fewer depressive symptoms and less fluctuation in manic symptoms. However, they did not report fewer manic symptoms.

This last finding is important because one potential drawback to CBT, as well as other skills-based therapies, is that it is more effective at reducing depression than reducing hypomanic symptoms (especially acute manic symptoms). In other words, mania and hypomania tend to respond better or more quickly to medication as opposed to therapeutic intervention. However, researchers and clinicians agree that *the best treatment for BPII is medication in addition to a skills-based therapy.*

In summary, CBT works to improve your mood by helping you change your thoughts and behaviors. In other words, *you have the ability to change your mood* by changing your thoughts and behaviors. This is a very important point and it's why we wrote this book: to give *you* a set of skills that will help you change your thoughts and behaviors so that you feel better. Table 2.2, at the end of this chapter, provides a summary of the therapy topics discussed in this book so that you may more easily navigate its chapters.

Dialectical Behavior Therapy

As discussed, CBT can be very effective in changing your negative thoughts and behaviors to help you feel better; however, what happens on days when you have trouble making these changes? Imagine a very difficult day—maybe you get into a car crash or someone you love falls ill. Or perhaps lots of minor stressors have piled up and you are feeling very overwhelmed. Might it be hard to change your negative thoughts or behaviors on these days? Yes! On these days, you need skills to help you *tolerate* not feeling well, as opposed to changing them.

Marsha Linehan, a psychologist at the University of Washington, recognized that the aspect of CBT that focuses on change may be invalidating, or difficult for people to embrace at times, so she developed dialectical behavior therapy (DBT; Linehan 1993b). DBT is similar to CBT because it is also structured and goal-oriented, but one key difference is that DBT emphasizes *accepting* overwhelming or painful emotions, without necessarily trying to change these emotions. The skills taught as part of DBT help people learn to handle distress in healthier ways and without losing control.

DBT skills are designed to help you accept your thoughts, feelings, and behaviors as they are without necessarily changing them. Of course, Dr. Linehan recognized the importance of changing negative thoughts, feelings, and behaviors too, but not without first being aware of them and validating their existence, or accepting them. (If this sounds confusing, you are not alone. These concepts can be difficult to understand, but they can be very helpful. We often think of acceptance as the first step in the change process, so in order to use CBT skills to change your negative thoughts and unhealthy behaviors, it might be wise to practice some DBT acceptance skills first. For this reason, we devote the next chapter to the DBT skill of acceptance.)

DBT has been shown to help people have fewer suicidal thoughts and require fewer psychiatric hospitalizations (Linehan et al. 2006; Linehan et al. 1999; Verheul et al. 2003). DBT was originally developed to help individuals with borderline personality disorder. However, it has been adapted to successfully treat other conditions, such as eating disorders (e.g., Safer, Telch, and Agras 2001;

Telch, Agras, and Linehan 2001), suicidality (Rathus and Miller 2002), and depression (Lynch et al. 2003). We the authors of this book, along with our colleagues, have also started using DBT skills in the MGH Bipolar Clinic and Research Program, with promising early results (Eisner et al. 2011). A very small pilot study of 10 people also found DBT to be useful for bipolar disorder (Goldstein et al. 2007). For these reasons, we include several DBT skills in this book to help you manage your BPII (see table 2.2).

Mindfulness-Based Cognitive Therapy

Drs. Zindel Segal, Mark Williams, and John Teasdale created mindfulness-based cognitive therapy (MBCT) to address recurrent depressive episodes (Segal, Williams, and Teasdale 2002). Formally, MBCT is an eight-week program that combines principles of CBT and mindfulness. Mindfulness involves focusing your attention on the present moment. Thus, MBCT aims to increase your awareness of unwanted thoughts, feelings, and body sensations so that you do not avoid them but accept them, and you learn to respond to them in healthier, or less negative, ways.

So far, evidence suggests that MBCT is helpful in preventing depressive episodes for people who have already had three or more depressive episodes (Ma and Teasdale 2004; Teasdale et al. 2000). In these studies, of the individuals who had experienced several episodes, those receiving MBCT were nearly twice as likely to feel better (e.g., MBCT reduced the chance of relapse from 78% to 36%). Recent evidence suggests that MBCT may also be helpful for BPII. Our colleagues at MGH have conducted small studies examining aspects of MBCT for bipolar disorder, with promising results (Deckersbach et al. 2012). Thus, we include several skills from MBCT in this book, namely acceptance and mindfulness-based techniques, to help you manage your BPII, as well as your anxiety (see table 2.2).

Family-Focused Treatment

An expert in the treatment of bipolar disorder, Dr. David Miklowitz, recognized how family stress can impact individuals with this disorder. Dr. Miklowitz and his colleagues developed a skills-based therapy, called family-focused treatment (FFT), to reduce stress in the home environment. Specifically, FFT seeks to improve communication, understanding, and support within the family through psychoeducation, communication enhancement, and problem-solving training (Miklowitz and Goldstein 1997).

FFT requires the involvement of at least one family member. It begins with helping clients understand how the family system, or the interactions within the family, may improve or worsen symptoms of depression or hypomania. FFT therapists try to identify ways to reduce "expressed emotion," defined as critical, hostile, or over-involved attitudes and behaviors, among family members. A key skill taught in FFT is how families can become more aware of expressed emotion and how family members can reduce levels of expressed emotion toward the person with bipolar disorder. FFT therapists also work with families to educate them on the nature of bipolar disorder, bipolar treatment, and ways that they can best support their affected member.

Adolescents and adults with bipolar disorder who received the skills taught as part of FFT had fewer mood episodes, longer periods of feeling well, and greater improvements in depressive symptoms compared to bipolar individuals who did not receive FFT (Miklowitz et al. 2000). Evidence also suggests that FFT may help people with bipolar disorder recover more quickly from their depressive symptoms (Miklowitz et al. 2008). Although we do not devote a chapter to FFT, we will discuss effective communication skills, particularly with friends and family, in chapter 11, as indicated in table 2.2.

Interpersonal and Social Rhythm Therapy

Interpersonal and social rhythm therapy (IPSRT) is based on the idea that a structured daily routine can minimize symptoms of depression (Ehlers, Frank, and Kupfer 1988) and reduce symptoms of hypomania (Grandin, Alloy, and Abramson 2006). Specifically, this theory suggests that life stress can trigger disruptions in your time cues, or activities that you structure your day around, such as meals, exercise, naps, or work. These disruptions in your time cues then disrupt your overall daily routine, which can cause biological changes in your body, such as fluctuations in your temperature, sleep drive, or hormone levels. It is suspected that these biological changes can then lead to episodes of depression, and possibly hypomania as well.

For most people, disruptions in routine are simply annoying, but for someone with BPII, these types of disruptions may actually lead to depressive or hypomanic symptoms. In addition, research has found that individuals with bipolar disorder have more difficulty than the average person in maintaining a regular schedule (Shen et al. 2008). Does this ring true for you? During times of stress, is it harder for you to maintain a daily schedule? How do you feel when you have no daily structure or routine? Perhaps you oversleep, skip meals, watch TV late at night, or overeat. How do these feelings and behaviors affect your mood?

In short, daily routine is particularly vital for people with BPII because a lack of structure may cause mood episodes. Unfortunately, you may be less likely to keep a daily routine because you have BPII. IPSRT is a skills-based psychotherapy that addresses this issue. IPSRT focuses on recognizing the association of stress and mood, stabilizing daily routines (i.e., social rhythms), and identifying and managing affective symptoms. In addition, it teaches skills that help resolve interpersonal problems (Frank 2005; Frank, Swartz, and Kupfer 2000). We will cover some of the skills from IPSRT in chapter 5 (see table 2.2). Specifically, we will review strategies for increasing the amount of structure and maintaining a healthy balance of activities in your daily routine.

Psychoeducation

The skills-based therapies discussed thus far (i.e., CBT, DBT, MBCT, FFT, and IPSRT) all include elements of educating and informing the client, but several researchers in Spain have developed a treatment for bipolar disorder that is primarily focused on teaching you about your illness, called psychoeducation (PE; Colom et al. 2003). PE differs from other therapies in that it views bipolar disorder as a predominantly biological illness (e.g., caused by genetic abnormalities in brain structure and function) and therefore focuses more heavily on your knowledge of medication compliance. Additionally, PE does not utilize other skills, such as actively changing your thoughts and behaviors (i.e., CBT), increasing your acceptance (i.e., DBT), using mind/body techniques (i.e., MBCT), decreasing expressed emotion in your family (i.e., FFT), or changing your daily routine (i.e., IPSRT), and is typically administered in a group format consisting of twenty-one sessions.

PE has proven quite helpful for individuals with bipolar disorder. For example, in one study, participants who received PE had fewer bipolar relapses and more days feeling well (i.e., without bipolar symptoms) than a control group (individuals not receiving PE). This highlights the importance of learning about your illness. The PE treatment group also had fewer depressive episodes during the study than the control group, but not fewer hypomanic or manic episodes (Colom et al. 2003).

Table 2.2. Therapy Topics Covered in This Book

Topic	Chapter	Primary Therapy(s)	Summary
Education about BPII	1	PE	Increase your understanding of the signs and symptoms of depression and hypomania.
Education about BPII treatments	2	All	Get an overview of treatment strategies for BPII.
Acceptance of having BPII	3	DBT, MBCT	Decrease judgment of your thoughts, feelings, and behaviors. Reduce your denial about having BPII.
Education about depression	4	PE	Increase your understanding of what triggers or causes your depression.
Monitoring logs for depression	4	CBT	Learn your specific triggers for depression and how to monitor them.
Cognitive restructuring for depression	5	CBT	Learn how to recognize and change your negative thinking.
Behavioral activation	5	CBT	Increase your daily activity level and improve your mood.
Daily routine/schedule regularity	5	CBT, IPSRT	Learn the importance of maintaining a daily routine and how to establish a healthy routine.
Relapse prevention for depression	5	CBT	Create a plan to decrease the likelihood of having another depressive episode.
Distress tolerance	6	DBT	Learn to "sit with," or tolerate, difficult emotions.
Mindfulness	6	DBT, MBCT	Learn how to be in the present moment to decrease your judgments.
Eating well	6	CBT	Learn how eating well can help your mood and overall health.
Exercise	6	CBT, IPSRT	Learn the importance of exercise in staying well mentally and physically.
Education about hypomania	7	PE	Increase your understanding of what triggers or causes your hypomania.

Monitoring logs for hypomania	7	CBT	Learn your specific triggers for hypomania and how to monitor them.
Cognitive restructuring for hypomania	8	CBT	Learn how to recognize and change your hyperpositive thinking.
Sleep hygiene	8	CBT, IPSRT	Learn how to maintain a regular sleep routine.
Impulsivity	8	CBT, DBT	Gain skills to help you act less impulsively.
Relapse prevention for hypomania	8	CBT	Create a plan to decrease the likelihood of having another hypomanic episode.
Education about fear versus anxiety	9	CBT, PE	Increase your understanding of what anxiety is and how it is similar to and different from fear.
The role of anxiety	9	CBT	Understand the causes of anxiety.
Education about anxiety disorders	9	CBT, PE	Understand what determines an anxiety disorder.
Exposure	10	CBT	Learn to expose yourself to feared objects or contexts to overcome your anxiety.
Deep breathing exercises	10	DBT, CBT, MBCT	Practice deep breathing techniques to help you relax.
Body scan	10	MBCT	Learn to focus your attention on bodily sensations instead of unpleasant thoughts and feelings.
Imagery	10	DBT, CBT, MBCT	Use your imagination to help you relax.
Speaking to other people about BPII	11	FFT, CBT	Learn how to speak to others about your BPII.
Communication skills	11	FFT, CBT, DBT	Learn how to be more effective when communicating with others and how to manage unexpected reactions.
Increasing your support	11	FFT	Identify what type of support is most useful to you and from whom.
Making a plan to manage your BPII	12	CBT	Make a Personalized Wellness Plan with your friends and family to carefully monitor and manage your BPII.

Conclusion

At this point, you may be wondering why we have not chosen to focus on just one of the skills-based therapies (i.e., CBT, DBT, MBCT, FFT, IPSRT, or PE). The answer comes in part from a very large study funded by the National Institute of Mental Health, called the Systematic Treatment Enhancement Program for Bipolar Disorder (STEP-BD) (Sachs et al. 2003). This study enrolled almost 5,000 people with mostly bipolar I or II disorder. If during the course of the study participants became depressed (and were taking a mood stabilizer), they were then randomly assigned to CBT, FFT, IPSRT, or a control group (i.e., three 50-minute sessions of PE). Two hundred and ninety-three people participated in this smaller STEP study, and it was discovered that all three treatment groups (i.e., FFT, CBT, and IPSRT) had higher recovery rates, as well as faster recovery times, than the control group (Miklowitz, Otto, Frank, Reilly-Harrington, Kogan, et al. 2007; Miklowitz, Otto, Frank, Reilly-Harrington, Wisniewski, et al. 2007). This study also did not find any differences in recovery time between the three skills-based therapies, but larger studies are needed to confirm this. In short, the good news is that each of these interventions was helpful in treating bipolar disorder, but it appears that we do not know whether one treatment is better than another, particularly for BPII.

Thus, we have chosen specific skills across these different treatments that we believe will help you manage your BPII (see table 2.2), as opposed to selecting just one therapy. For this reason, we suggest that you take some time to complete exercise 2.1 before reading further.

Exercise 2.1.   How Skills-Based Therapies May Help You

Taking ten minutes to complete this worksheet now will help you make the best use of this book. Although we believe that all the skills in this book will at least be somewhat helpful for your BPII, there may be certain skills that will be particularly important for you to practice or seek support in using. For example, if you identify that lack of structure, or daily routine, is a particular problem in managing your depression, then you may want to spend extra time on the skills taught in chapter 5 and have a close friend or relative read this chapter as well. Once you have finished this exercise, you can look back to table 2.2 to see which chapters cover which skills.

The symptoms of BPII that bother me the most are:

_____

_____

_____

My symptoms seem to be particularly triggered by:

_____

_____

_____

Based on my symptoms, my triggers, and the information in this chapter, I believe that the following skills will be most helpful for me:

_____

_____

_____

I believe that these skills will be most helpful for me because:

_____

_____

_____

Three people who could help me learn and/or practice these skills are:

_____

_____

_____

Chapter Summary:

- BPII is the result of both genetic (biological) and environmental factors.

- Skills-based therapy in conjunction with medication is the most effective treatment for BPII.

- This book teaches skills from proven skills-based therapies.

- Certain skills may be particularly helpful for you.

CHAPTER 3

Applying Acceptance to Bipolar II Disorder

To begin this chapter, we encourage you to ask yourself the following question: To what extent do I accept being a person who has bipolar II disorder (BPII)? *Acceptance* of your BPII diagnosis does not necessarily mean that you like having BPII, nor does it mean that you have given up on trying to manage your illness. Instead, accepting your BPII diagnosis is the first step to making positive changes in your life. Thus, before we begin discussing specific skills to help you change the way your BPII affects you, we first want to help you accept having BPII.

Acceptance Defined

Acceptance is often described as when we give our "assent," or approval, for a certain situation. In the field of psychology, acceptance is defined as not necessarily "assenting" or "giving in to" the reality of the situation, but just seeing reality for what it is. The proverb "it is what it is" captures the essence of this concept. Acceptance is not an excuse to doing nothing about your situation; rather it is a first (and necessary) step to making changes in your life.

Imagine that Pete, a twenty-nine-year-old store clerk in New York City, must move in with a roommate because he can no longer afford to live on his own. Pete is very upset about this and thinks, *I just can't believe that I have to have a roommate after living alone for five years. This is so unfair!* As a result, Pete is angry and irritable toward his new roommate, Joe, and does not make efforts to live peacefully with him. For example, he does not clean up after himself, he comes home late, and he plays his music loudly.

Now, imagine an alternative situation. In this situation, Pete is still disappointed that he must live with a roommate, but in this scenario he says to himself: *Having a roommate is really annoying, but at least this will help me financially. So I'll do the best that I can to share my space, and hopefully I can have my own place again soon.* As a result, Pete tries to live peacefully with Joe by cleaning up after himself, being quiet, and generally trying to compromise and solve problems with Joe.

This second situation is an example of practicing acceptance. When you practice acceptance, you recognize your current situation for what it is and, though you may not like it, you try to make the best of it.

Why Acceptance Is Important

At this point, you may be thinking, *It's one thing to practice acceptance about living with a roommate, but it is very different to practice acceptance with regard to living with a chronic mental illness that does not currently have a cure.* You are absolutely right. Practicing acceptance *is* difficult, particularly when the stakes are high. In short, it is much more difficult to accept things that you do not like, and most people do not like living with BPII.

Remember that practicing acceptance does not mean that you like or enjoy having BPII. In the preceding examples, do you think that Pete is looking forward to having a roommate? No, not at all. The difference between the first and second scenarios is that in the second, Pete has decided to acknowledge that living with a roommate is his reality, as opposed to denying or not accepting it. We argue that working toward accepting your BPII is vital to making positive changes in your life. This is similar to how Pete will likely better manage his living situation after accepting that he must live with Joe.

Given that this idea of acceptance can be difficult to understand, let's consider another example:

• Michael

Michael, age fifty-five, has always practiced a healthy lifestyle. He eats a well-balanced diet, exercises four days per week, and has never smoked. However, for several months now, he has noticed a worsening cough, shortness of breath, and wheezing. He finally goes to see his doctor, who, after a series of tests, informs him that he has lung cancer and must start treatment immediately. Michael is devastated and also angry and says to himself, How could this happen to me? This is so unfair! I've always lived a healthy lifestyle. These tests must be wrong!

After a few days, in which Michael talks to his friends, family, and doctors, his anger subsides and he makes an important realization: in order to start treatment for his cancer, he must acknowledge the fact that he indeed has cancer. If he were to continue denying this reality, he would likely not seek or adhere to his treatment and thus make his situation worse. So he starts telling himself, I am very sad that I have this illness, but I will do everything that I need to do to try to make it better. *He reads all the information he can find on lung cancer, carefully follows doctors' orders, and joins a local cancer support group. Although he is certainly not happy to have this diagnosis, he recognizes it for what it is, which allows him to manage it as best he can. In short, Michael is practicing acceptance.*

How far along are you in accepting your BPII? To answer this question, try the following exercise.

Exercise 3.1. Self-Test: Acceptance of Bipolar II Disorder

Circle the number that best indicates how much you agree with each of the following statements or how often it is true for you.

	Not at All	Rarely/ A Little	Sometimes/ Somewhat	Often/ Very Much
I ask myself why I have to have BPII.	1	2	3	4
I try to pretend that I am "normal" or do not have BPII.	1	2	3	4
I am angry that I have BPII.	1	2	3	4
I think that it is not fair that I have BPII.	1	2	3	4
I believe that I have been cursed or punished by having BPII.	1	2	3	4
I try to forget about having BPII or ignore that I have it.	1	2	3	4
I tell myself that I do not actually have BPII.	1	2	3	4
I say to myself that there is nothing that I can do about my BPII.	1	2	3	4

Scoring. Add up the numbers that you circled. If you scored between 24 and 32, chances are that you are having trouble accepting your BPII. If so, these next few sections will be particularly important.

How Acceptance May Help You Manage Bipolar II Disorder

Before we move on to strategies that will help you practice acceptance, we'd like you to better understand how this concept can relate to you and your BPII. So let's consider Lori and Steve, who illustrate two different ways of dealing with BPII.

• Lori and Steve

Lori, age twenty, has been struggling in her college courses because her BPII symptoms make it difficult for her to concentrate in class and do her homework. As a result, her grades have fallen, and she is at risk of failing several of her courses. This is very frustrating for Lori because until her symptoms worsened, she had always performed very well in school. Lori tells herself that it is "no big deal" and that she will be okay if she just ignores these symptoms. Thus, Lori pretends that she does not have the disorder. She does not tell her close friends, family, or teachers, and she decides not to seek any treatment. She also does not change her study habits, but instead tells herself that she can just try harder and force herself to do her homework. Consequently, she fails two of her courses and must retake them, delaying her graduation date.

Lori's classmate, Steve, also has BPII. He, like Lori, begins to struggle in school due to his symptoms and is very frustrated by this as well. However, Steve tells himself, This is a problem and I need to deal with it. Thus, Steve decides to tell his friends and family, who then encourage him to discuss his illness with his professors and academic advisor. Steve also decides that he could benefit from learning from other people with BPII and thus joins a support group. In addition, he seeks help from his therapist and psychiatrist. Collectively, these resources help him deal with his mood symptoms. Furthermore, he learns to change his study habits such that he takes frequent breaks, does not study too late at night, and studies with a friend, which helps him stay focused. As a result, his grades improve and he manages to pass all of his courses.

Who do you think will manage his or her BPII better—Lori or Steve? We hope that the obvious answer is Steve. Why do you think that he will be more successful? There are many things that may help Steve manage his BPII, but notice that the first thing he does when he discovers that he has the disorder is tell himself, *This is a problem and I need to deal with it.* In contrast, Lori denies her illness and says that it is "no big deal." Neither person likes having BPII, but Steve acknowledges that he has it and thus takes appropriate steps to manage it. In short, Steve practices acceptance and Lori does not. Notice that this is similar to how Michael decided to accept his diagnosis of cancer: he chose to accept the fact that he had an illness that he needed to manage. This is why we began this chapter by stating that acceptance of your BPII is the first step to managing it.

Practicing Acceptance

Clients often ask us, "How do you practice acceptance?" and "What does it look like when someone is practicing acceptance?" To answer these questions, think about how you are already practicing acceptance in your life. For example, there are many situations that you may find easy to accept, such as eating a meal at your favorite restaurant, getting a promotion at work, or winning a prize!

You may also be practicing acceptance with some things that you do not like, such as rainy days or getting stuck in traffic. Maybe one day while in traffic you just told yourself: *This is okay. I am in traffic. This does not have to ruin my day; I can choose to accept that this is the way the traffic is today.* If you have not done this, try saying these things to yourself the next time that you are in traffic…. You are now practicing acceptance!

Exercise 3.2. Steps to Practicing Acceptance

We suggest three ways to practice acceptance. First, notice what you are already accepting. What do you tell yourself in these situations? Perhaps you recognize how immersed you are in the pleasant experience or you recognize that even an unpleasant situation (e.g., a rainy day) has not derailed you. You may observe how present you are in the moment or how little your mind wanders or is distracted during these moments. These are indicators that you are not fighting or denying the situation. In other words, these are indicators that you are accepting your current situation. Second, think about the situations that you may sometimes have difficulty accepting. Finally, think about situations that you have not been able to accept. We give examples of these steps in the following table, as well as a column for you to add your own examples.

	Our Examples	Your Examples
Step 1: Identify situations that you are already accepting (you are able to acknowledge that these are or could be your realities).	Going on vacation Eating a favorite meal Making a new friend Paying taxes Receiving a nice e-mail Getting a salary raise Going to the dentist Cleaning the house Moving to a new home/apartment Getting married A rainy day	
Step 2: Identify situations that you are having difficulty accepting (some days you are able to accept these realities and some days you are not able to).	Having to wear eyeglasses Eating healthy foods Getting into an argument with a friend Receiving an unfriendly e-mail Salary cuts Getting older A raise in rent Having a roommate Needing to exercise	
Step 3: Identify situations that you are currently not able to accept or try to deny (every day you are not able to accept these realities).	Not liking my job Getting divorced Having financial trouble The death of a loved one Having BPII Getting fired Having a car accident	

Now you are ready to start practicing acceptance of the things that are difficult to accept. It's best to start with situations that you only have some difficulty accepting, such as the examples that you listed in step 2, rather than situations that are very difficult for you to accept or acknowledge (or examples you listed in step 3). For example, to practice acceptance about being stuck in traffic, you may want to begin by observing other drivers. Are some drivers exhibiting "road rage" or driving aggressively? Do you think these drivers are effectively practicing acceptance? In contrast, how about the driver who seems to be savoring his coffee or singing along to the radio—is he perhaps more likely to be practicing acceptance? Next, try to imagine what you could tell yourself to be more like the people who are practicing acceptance in their car. Perhaps you could say *Traffic often happens on Mondays at 8:00 a.m.; It is what it is*, or *This is my reality*. We list more possible accepting statements in the following table.

General Accepting Statement	Accepting Statement for BPII
"This situation is a card that I have been dealt. I will manage it better if I acknowledge that I have it."	"I have BPII. I will manage this disorder better if I acknowledge that I have it and seek ways to manage it."
"I may not like this situation, but it is here and a part of my reality. My options to deal with it are…."	"I don't necessarily like having BPII, but I have it. I have options for dealing with it, such as using the skills in this book."
"Choosing not to think about this situation will not help it go away. It may only give me *temporary* relief."	"Ignoring the fact that I have BPII will not make it go away. It may actually hurt me in the long run as I'll be less likely to do something to help it."
"Other people may have this same situation. I can learn how they have dealt with it."	"Other people have BPII. I can learn how they try to manage it as well as gain support for what I'm doing to manage my illness."
"Acting as though everything is normal, or as though this situation did not occur, will not mean that this situation will go away or never have happened."	"Trying to 'act normal' or as if I don't have BPII, particularly around my close friends and family, won't help me gain others' support and understanding, and it could hurt me."

Note. BPII = Bipolar II Disorder.

Try saying these statements, also called coping statements or mantras, to yourself. You may notice when saying these mantras that you are more likely to do something to increase the tolerability of the situation. This is evidence that you are practicing acceptance!

After practicing acceptance by using coping statements with the situations that you mildly dislike, or have only some trouble accepting, try applying these coping statements to the situations that you are having much more difficulty accepting (e.g., examples you listed in step 3). For example, you have lost a loved one and do not want to face the reality that this person is no longer in your life. How does it feel to try to pretend that this person is still in your life? Perhaps you say things such as "I can't believe _____ has died" or "My life will never go on now." Our guess is that these thoughts have not helped you feel better. In contrast, try telling yourself that you miss this person, but he or she is now gone, so what are you going to do about it? Perhaps you will decide to join a grief support group to help you process losing this person or increase your acceptance of your loss. You could also decide to start a new hobby to keep yourself busy or sign up for a social activity to meet a new person. Using coping statements and then taking actions like these can increase your acceptance of your loss. We suspect that by accepting your reality, you will be more likely to do something to improve your situation and thus feel better. These same concepts apply to learning to accept your BPII.

In teaching the concept of acceptance to our clients over the years, we have heard many interesting accepting statements. For example, one client, a basketball fan, found that a quote by former Boston Celtics coach Rick Pitino really illustrated the idea of acceptance for him. To understand how this quote is an accepting statement, we'll give you a little background on the Celtics. As you may know, Larry Bird, Kevin McHale, and Robert Parish, known as the "Big Three," were outstanding Celtics players in the 1980s. Together, they amassed 62,460 points, 30,811 rebounds, and three NBA championships for the Celtics. However, by March 2000 (after the "Big Three" had retired), the Boston Celtics were having a tough season. Referring to the expectations of Celtics fans and the media, coach Rick Pitino challenged the public and the players to let go of the past and focus on the future with the following statement:

Larry Bird is not walking through that door, fans. Kevin McHale is not walking through that door, and Robert Parish is not walking through that door. And if you expect them to walk through that door, they're going to be gray and old. What we are is young, exciting, hard-working, and we're going to improve. People don't realize that, and as soon as they realize those three guys are not coming through that door, the better this town will be.... I wish we had $90 million under the salary cap. I wish we could buy the world. We can't; the only thing we can do is work hard. (Keefe 2009)

Essentially, what Rick Pitino is saying is that the fans and the players need to accept that the team is not what it used to be. Once they do that, the team can work on improving their game. For our client, this statement really hit home, and so he used it as one of his accepting statements. He wrote it on note cards that he put on the dashboard of his car so that he saw it every day. He would also say it to himself when he had difficulty accepting certain aspects of his BPII, or when he got caught up in reminiscing about the "good old" days before he developed BPII.

Exercise 3.3.   Creating Accepting Statements

Spend some time trying to come up with your own accepting statements.

Using the example accepting statements in the previous exercise as a guide, write your own accepting statements for your BPII. If you say one of these new statements out loud and don't feel any differently, keep trying other ideas. If you need help, friends and relatives might be able to give you ideas; ask them how they cope with difficult situations and what they tell themselves.

Statement 1

_____

_____

_____

Statement 2

_____

_____

_____

Statement 3

_____

_____

_____

Statement 4

_____

_____

_____

Statement 5

_____

_____

_____

One important thing to remember is that acceptance is a process. It is not a skill that you can master overnight, so be patient. Acceptance can be a very different way of viewing your BPII, so it may take you time to be able to fully apply acceptance toward it. When trying to accept aspects of your BPII, it may be helpful to think about accepting it for just a certain amount of time per day.

For example, you may find that you can accept the fact that you tend to get depressed every winter for only five minutes at first. Over time, you can gradually increase the amount of time that you accept being depressed, until eventually you feel as if you accept this reality most of or all the time.

You may find it helpful to photocopy your completed exercise 3.3, "Creating Accepting Statements," so that you can have your accepting statements available to you at all times. Or write these statements on note cards (like our Boston Celtics fan), put them on a blackboard, or enter them as reminders into your smartphone. Essentially, you want your accepting statements to be in places where you can see them every day. Once you think that you are learning to accept your BPII (redo exercise 3.1, "Self-Test: Acceptance of Bipolar II Disorder," if you are not sure!), you are ready to use the rest of this book to begin to monitor and manage your illness.

Chapter Summary:

- Accepting your BPII does not mean giving into it or doing nothing about it.

- Accepting your BPII means recognizing that you have an illness so that you can be proactive about monitoring and managing it.

- It can be difficult to accept the things that you do not like, such as having BPII.

- There are ways that you can practice accepting difficult situations, such as having BPII.

- Increasing your acceptance of your BPII will increase the likelihood that you will be proactive about monitoring and managing it.

PART 2

How to Manage Depressive Episodes

As discussed in chapter 1, depression is a defining characteristic of bipolar II disorder (BPII); in order to receive a diagnosis of BPII, you must have experienced at least one episode of major depression. Depression is in fact often the biggest problem for people with BPII. By definition, major depression has a negative impact on your life and causes interference or problems with managing life, work, or relationships. Therefore, it is extremely important that you thoroughly understand what your depression looks like and how to manage it. In this section of the workbook, we will help you recognize the symptoms and triggers of your depression. We will also discuss tools for monitoring your depressive symptoms and provide specific suggestions for coping with your depression.

CHAPTER 4

Recognizing the Symptoms of Bipolar II Depression

In the prologue to her bestselling memoir of depression *Prozac Nation: Young and Depressed in America*, Elizabeth Wurtzel says: "I start to feel like I can't maintain the façade any longer, that I may just start to show through. And I wish I knew what was wrong. Maybe something about how stupid my whole life is. I don't know" (Wurtzel 1994, 1). Later in the book, she relates her depression in the following way: "Why does the rest of the world put up with the hypocrisy, the need to put a happy face on sorrow, the need to keep on keeping on?…I don't know the answer, I just know that I can't. I don't want any more [difficulties], I don't want any more of this try, try again stuff. I just want out. I've had it. I am so tired. I am twenty and I am already exhausted" (293).

While everyone experiences depression differently, Wurtzel's words illustrate how depression can change your perceptions of yourself, your world, and your future. It can make you feel hopeless. Depression can make you feel exhausted, even if you are sleeping more than usual. It can make it hard to get out of bed in the morning and to accomplish everyday tasks, such as getting dressed or doing chores around your house. Many people with bipolar disorder also experience irritability when they feel depressed (Deckersbach et al. 2004).

The first part of this chapter will help you identify the ways in which you experience symptoms of depression.

Exercise 4.1.   Self-Test: Symptoms of Depression

Think about how you have been feeling over the past two weeks, and ask yourself the following questions. Circle yes for a symptom even if you only agree with one of the questions. In other words, you don't have to endorse all the questions in order to circle yes for that symptom.

1. **Sad mood.** Am I feeling blue, down in the dumps, or crying more often than usual? Do I feel as if a dark cloud is hanging over me?

   Yes   No

2. **Loss of interest.** Am I less interested in doing things that I have enjoyed in the past? Do I have to push myself to get together with friends? Do I care less about my goals or dreams?

   Yes   No

3. **Feelings of guilt or worthlessness.** Am I getting down on myself or feeling very self-critical? Do I find myself thinking over and over about mistakes that I've made? Am I blaming myself for many things? Am I having feelings of worthlessness? Do I feel as though I deserve to be punished for something?

   Yes   No

4. **Energy.** Am I feeling tired or exhausted most of the time? Is it hard to find the energy to get through daily routines?

   Yes   No

5. **Concentration.** Is it hard to focus on reading, having a conversation, or watching a television show? Is it taking longer than usual to complete tasks that require focus, such as balancing my checkbook or composing an e-mail? Is it hard to make even small decisions, such as what to eat or which clothes to wear?

   Yes   No

6. **Appetite.** Has my appetite increased? Am I overeating or bingeing on certain foods? Has my appetite decreased? Have I lost interest in food? Is food less enjoyable to me? Have others had to remind me or encourage me to eat?

   Yes   No

7. **Movement.** Do I feel as though I am moving in slow motion? Am I feeling restless or agitated? Is it hard for me to sit still?

   Yes   No

8. **Sleep.** Am I having trouble falling asleep at night? Am I tossing and turning or having restless, interrupted sleep? Am I waking up earlier in the morning than necessary? Am I oversleeping and having difficulty getting out of bed? Am I napping during the day?

   Yes   No

9. **Thoughts of death or suicide.*** Am I having thoughts that life is not worth living? Am I thinking more about death? Am I wishing that I would fall asleep and not wake up? Am I making any plans to hurt or kill myself? Have I made any preparations to die?

Yes   No

* Suicide is a very real risk for people with BPII. You must immediately go to an emergency room, call 911, or page your doctor if you answered yes to the preceding question and/or are at immediate risk of hurting yourself. We will talk more about these types of suicidal thoughts later in this chapter, as well as create a plan for managing suicidal thoughts in chapter 12.

Understanding Your Answers

Now that you have completed the test, there are a few more questions to ask yourself before you can understand your symptoms:

Have I experienced either symptom 1 (sad mood) or symptom 2 (loss of interest) consistently over the past two weeks?

Yes   No

Have I experienced at least *four* of the other symptoms (symptoms 3–9) consistently over the past two weeks?

Yes   No

Have these symptoms interfered significantly with my ability to function, work, or interact with other people over the past two weeks?

Yes   No

If you responded yes to these three questions, you may currently be in an episode of major depression. If you do meet criteria for a current episode of major depression, it is even more important for you to work with a doctor and/or therapist, in addition to using the skills you will learn in this book. Even if you do not meet the criteria for a full-blown episode of depression at this time, you may have experienced an episode of major depression in the past, and therefore the skills provided in this book are likely to be helpful to you. Furthermore, even if you are not currently experiencing a major depressive episode, you may still be experiencing some depressive symptoms that are causing you distress.

Many people with bipolar II disorder (BPII) experience ongoing symptoms of depression that ebb and flow over time. The next section discusses some issues that are particularly important to your understanding of depression specifically in people with BPII.

Unique Characteristics of Bipolar II Depression

A thorough understanding of your depressive symptoms, triggers, and intervention strategies is essential. This section focuses on unique characteristics of depression in people with BPII, because these symptoms may be particularly relevant for you.

Individuals with BPII may be particularly likely to experience frequent depressive episodes and/or changes of mood, more so than individuals with bipolar I disorder (Baek et al. 2011).

In terms of symptoms, individuals with BPII may be more likely to experience guilty feelings and physical feelings of agitation during depression (Baek et al. 2011).

Individuals with BPII may also be more likely to have what are called *atypical features of depression*. The following characteristics are found in atypical depression (Brugue et al. 2008):

- Having depression that momentarily lifts in response to positive news or pleasant events but returns later

- Increases in appetite and weight gain

- Increased amounts of sleep

- Heavy, leaden feelings in arms and legs

- Fears of interpersonal rejection that interfere with relationships

Individuals with BPII have a high likelihood of having suicidal thoughts (Baek et al. 2011) and attempting suicide (Serretti et al. 2002). Thus, we want you to be especially aware of any thoughts of suicide. It is best to catch these thoughts early so that you can begin to take active steps to cope with or manage them. The following factors have been shown to worsen suicidal thoughts in people with bipolar disorder (Gonda et al. 2012):

- Aggressive/impulsive personality traits

- Negative events that occurred early in life (separation from loved ones; emotional, physical, or sexual abuse)

- Stressful current life events

- A family history of mood disorders and/or suicide in close relatives

- Onset of bipolar disorder at a young age (fifteen years or younger)

- Recent onset of bipolar disorder

- A long history of untreated bipolar disorder

- Severe depression and multiple episodes of depression

- A prior suicide attempt

- Current suicidal thoughts, attempts, or plans

- Rapidly changing mood, otherwise known as *rapid cycling*

- Agitation, or physical restlessness

- Insomnia

- Anxiety

- Hopelessness, guilt, or seeing few reasons for living

- *Psychotic features:* hearing voices or seeing things that are not there

- Atypical features of depression (as defined in the preceding section)

- Substance use and abuse

- Serious medical illness

- Lack of medical treatment

- Lack of family or social support

- *Personality disorders*, or long-standing patterns of behavior that interfere with relationships and functioning

While the next chapter will discuss ways for you to cope with your depression and suicidal thoughts, we'd like you to consider these risk factors for suicide in people with BPII and think about how they may apply to you. In our clinical practices, we routinely use the worksheet in exercise 4.2 to help our clients think about the ways they can keep themselves safe. We encourage you to complete exercise 4.2, even if you have never had thoughts of suicide, because it is always better to have a plan for dealing with them in case they develop. Doing this now will also be very helpful when you create your Personalized Wellness Plan in chapter 12.

Exercise 4.2.   Checklist: Ways to Stay Safe from Suicide

Place a check mark next to all the strategies that you plan to use or think you would be most likely to use to keep yourself safe from suicide:

_____   I will notify my doctor immediately if I am having serious thoughts about suicide.

_____   I will be as honest as possible when my doctor or therapist asks me whether I am feeling safe.

_____   I will contact a friend or family member if I am feeling at risk of suicide.

_____ I will call 911 if I am having immediate thoughts of suicide.

_____ I will call a suicide hotline if I am feeling at risk. (The National Suicide Prevention Lifeline is available in the United States twenty-four hours a day at 1-800-273-8255.)

_____ I will attend all my therapy and medical appointments.

_____ I will contact someone from my faith community (e.g., minister, rabbi, or spiritual leader).

_____ I will ask a friend or family member to hold my extra medications for me if I am feeling at risk of overdosing on medication.

_____ I will limit my access to means of suicide (e.g., giving a firearm to a family member to hold for me).

_____ I will remember that depression can change my perceptions and that suicide is a final act that cannot be changed.

_____ I will make a list of and then review my reasons for living.

_____ I will avoid alcohol and recreational drugs.

Three Different Stories of Bipolar II Depression

As discussed previously in this chapter, depression can manifest in a variety of ways for people with BPII. These three stories illustrate how differently people can experience bipolar depression:

• Katie

Katie is a twenty-year-old college student who was recently diagnosed with BPII. For the past two weeks, she has been struggling with a relapse of depression following a breakup with her boyfriend. She has been missing her classes because she has had difficulty getting out of bed. In addition, she has been eating large amounts of candy and pizza and has gained weight. Her arms and legs feel weighed down, and she feels as if she is moving in slow motion. She is intensely self-critical about her weight and her appearance, and consequently, she has been avoiding all social interactions. She is convinced that her friends don't care about her anymore, even though they have been calling and trying to see her. She has been crying every day and has lost interest in most of the activities that she used to enjoy. She has even had some fleeting thoughts of suicide, although she has assured herself and her therapist that she would not do anything to kill herself.

• Jack

Jack is a forty-five-year-old sales manager who has struggled with BPII for many years. He has had long periods of feeling well and has been quite successful in his career. Since the death of his father last year, however, he feels empty and hollow and has not been able to express any emotion toward his wife and three children. He is still going to work, but he is sometimes intensely irritable with his colleagues. He recently got into trouble for yelling at a coworker during a meeting. He often feels agitated at work and paces around his office. He also has become increasingly stressed about his family's financial situation and the possibility of layoffs at work. He has a decreased appetite and has lost a significant amount of weight. He struggles with insomnia nightly, and others have commented that he looks exhausted. He sometimes contemplates suicide and wonders whether his wife and children would be better off without him.

• Martha

Martha is a fifty-eight-year-old artist who lives with her husband in a seaside community. She typically enjoys painting and socializing during the spring and summer months. She has experienced numerous hypomanic episodes in which she has produced many beautiful paintings and required very little sleep, working for hours at a time. Now that winter is approaching and the hours of daylight have diminished, she is starting to experience the familiar feelings of sadness and loneliness. Her mood lifts temporarily for a few hours when she receives a telephone call from one of her children. She has lost interest in painting and doubts her abilities and talents, even though her art has received much critical acclaim. She has withdrawn from her social life and spends much of her day in bed. She has to push herself to shower and to get dressed, and she has trouble completing even simple chores around the house. She has never sought treatment for her depression and has never been properly diagnosed, despite her husband's urging her to seek help for years.

While Katie, Jack, and Martha are all experiencing bipolar II depression, their symptoms look quite different and affect their lives in a variety of ways. It is important that you get very familiar with your unique symptoms—the ways in which *you* experience depression. This information will be important in the next chapter (chapter 5), which focuses on managing your depression.

It is also vital to identify the earliest warning signs of your depression so that you can seek help and use tools to help yourself *before* your symptoms develop into a full-blown episode. For example, some people may begin to eat slightly more than usual in the early stages of feeling depressed. The associated weight gain may lead to negative thoughts about their appearance and less social contact. Eventually, more symptoms of depression may emerge and a full-blown major depressive episode may begin.

In the next chapter, we will discuss tools and strategies for managing these early warning signs and taking action to prevent an episode from occurring.

Exercise 4.3.   Checklist: Your Early Warning Signs and Symptoms of Depression

Place a check mark next to all the following symptoms that apply to you when you are depressed, and circle those that are early warning signs (symptoms that you tend to experience either right before or at the very beginning of a depressive episode). Add any additional early warning signs or symptoms in the empty spaces.

_____ Feeling sad or blue	_____ Feeling guilty
_____ Crying	_____ Blaming myself for things
_____ Wanting to cry, but not being able to	_____ Doubting that others have feelings of love or affection for me
_____ Losing interest in things I usually enjoy	_____ Thinking that I am worthless
_____ Avoiding friends or avoiding social activities	_____ Thinking that I deserve to be punished
_____ Feeling less emotion toward loved ones	_____ Difficulty concentrating
_____ Increased cravings for foods	_____ Trouble reading
_____ Eating more food	_____ Trouble having conversations
_____ Gaining weight	_____ Trouble following the plot of a TV show
_____ Loss of appetite	_____ Hard time making decisions
_____ Less enjoyment of food	_____ Thinking about death
_____ Losing weight	_____ Wishing I would fall asleep and not wake up
_____ Eating less than usual	_____ Hurting myself
_____ Trouble falling asleep	_____ Thinking about ways to die
_____ Restless or disturbed sleep	_____ Making preparations to die
_____ Waking during the middle of the night	_____ Thinking that life is not worth living
_____ Waking up earlier than I want to	_____ Feeling irritable
_____ More sleepy than usual	_____ Increased impulsivity
_____ Oversleeping	_____ Getting into arguments

_____ Trouble getting out of bed		_____	Falling behind at work or school
_____ Napping		_____	Feeling anxious
_____ Being restless or agitated		_____	Difficulty with bathing or grooming
_____ Pacing		_____	Thinking my future is hopeless
_____ Having trouble sitting still		_____	Thinking the world is a bad place
_____ Feeling slowed down		_____	Hearing voices or seeing things that are not there
_____ Feeling very tired		_____	Reacting positively to good news, but then feeling sad
_____ Having low energy		_____	Feeling hollow or empty
_____ Arms or legs feeling heavy or weighed down		_____	Abrupt changes or shifts in mood
_____ Feeling numb		_____	Calling/seeing friends and family less often
_____ Feeling aggressive		_____	_____
_____ Using drugs or alcohol		_____	_____
_____ Being self-critical		_____	_____
_____ Trouble getting chores done at home			

You have taken an important step in reflecting on and understanding how you experience depression. In the next chapter, we will begin to discuss tools and strategies for alleviating and coping with these symptoms, but first we need to identify your triggers for depression.

Triggers for Depression

In addition to understanding your signs and symptoms of depression, it is very important that you become aware of your potential triggers or causes for depression. In the preceding stories of bipolar depression, you met Katie, Jack, and Martha. Each of them had some life events or circumstances that contributed to his or her depressive episode. For Katie, it was breaking up with her boyfriend. For Jack, it was the death of his father the year before. He was also facing some increased stress at work and the possibility of layoffs. In Martha's case, she experienced a seasonal pattern to her depression, which predictably occurred each winter. In this section, we discuss some of the potential triggers for depression in people with BPII.

Stress

Unfortunately, people's lives are filled with many stressors. For example, many people today are stressed about their financial situation. Coping with the burden of a medical illness, such as BPII, can also cause significant stress. The daily hassles of life (traffic, waiting in lines, rude people, and so on) can also contribute to depression. The constant connection to media and computers can also be quite stressful, because opportunities to be completely "unplugged," or shut down all of these sources of input, are rare.

One type of stress that is particularly likely to cause depression is an event that involves loss. Losing a relationship due to breakup, estrangement, or death is particularly likely to trigger depression in some individuals. Other people may be more vulnerable to the types of losses that limit their feelings of productivity or independence. Such individuals may be most prone to depression when laid off or when experiencing a setback at work.

Stressful life events may influence the onset and course of depression in people with bipolar disorder (Johnson 2005). Researchers have found that negative life events are associated with slower recovery from bipolar depression and increases in depression over time (Johnson and Miller 1997; Johnson et al. 2008). Reilly-Harrington, Alloy, Fresco, and Whitehouse (1999) examined individuals with bipolar disorders and found that the way those individuals processed or perceived negative life events had an impact on whether or not they became depressed in response to those stressors. So, your perceptions, thoughts, and attitudes can certainly impact how depressed you might become in response to negative events in your life.

In chapter 5, we will discuss ways to buffer the impact of stressful life events and decrease your risk of depression.

It's important to recognize that even positive life events, such as getting married, having a baby, graduating, or getting a big promotion can cause stress and precipitate depression. Anything that changes your daily routines can have a big impact on your mood.

Disruption to Your Schedule

Regulating your schedule through a daily pattern of consistent sleep/wake times, mealtimes, activity levels, and exercise can be enormously helpful in stabilizing your mood. Conversely, irregularity in daily routines has been associated with mood instability and mood episodes in bipolar disorder. All sorts of stressors and life changes can lead to lifestyle irregularity—moving to a new place, sustaining an injury that prevents exercise, staying up late to study for exams or meet a deadline, or changing work shifts.

Lifestyle regularity can be particularly challenging for individuals with BPII. In a study of college students, researchers found that students with a bipolar diagnosis reported fewer regular daily activities than the students with no diagnosis (Shen et al. 2008). They also found that students with less regularity to their routines were more likely to have a mood episode (depression or hypomania) sooner in the study.

Sleep is a critically important component of schedule regularity. Changes in sleep patterns (either sleeping too much or sleeping too little) can be both triggers and symptoms of depression. Try to maintain regular sleep patterns even when you start to feel depressed.

We will talk more about strategies for maintaining consistency in your daily routines later in this book. For now, keep in mind that a disruption in your usual routines can serve as a trigger for a mood episode.

Seasonal Changes

Individuals with BPII may be more susceptible to seasonal changes than individuals with other forms of bipolar disorder (Baek et al. 2011; Friedman et al. 2006). There has been some debate within psychology about the exact effects of seasonal changes on mood states. But, we've found that many of our clients report a greater risk of depression in the winter months, hypothetically due to decreased exposure to daylight. One study (Friedman et al. 2006) found increases in bipolar II depression in February and December, but also in June. Think about the effects, if any, that seasonal changes have on your own mood patterns.

Hormonal Changes

Hormonal changes can trigger or exacerbate depression in women with bipolar disorder. The majority of women with bipolar disorder report premenstrual exacerbation of depression (Dias et al. 2011; Payne et al. 2007). This is of particular importance to women with BPII, as *premenstrual dysphoric disorder* (a pattern of increased depression and interpersonal sensitivity around menstrual cycles) is more common in those with BPII than those with other forms of bipolar disorder (Choi et al. 2011; Kim, Czarkowski, and Epperson 2011). Keeping track of your menstrual cycle can be enormously helpful in predicting and coping with monthly mood shifts. The Daily Diary Card at the end of this chapter can help in this regard.

Women with bipolar disorder are also particularly at risk for depression after giving birth. In fact, women with bipolar disorder are at a significantly increased risk of psychiatric admission in the first three weeks after giving birth, as compared to women without bipolar disorder (Munk-Olsen et al. 2009). New fathers with bipolar disorder are also at increased risk for a mood episode (Pinheiro et al. 2011; Quevedo et al. 2011). Even though having a baby is a joyful event for most people, as you can probably imagine, it leads to a great deal of schedule disruption and sometimes a loss of productivity and independence.

Menopause can also be particularly challenging for women with bipolar disorder. An increased rate of depression has been shown for women with bipolar disorder who are going through menopause (Marsh, Ketter, and Rasgon 2009).

Family Communication Patterns

Researchers who examine family stress have found that certain types of communication patterns between family members can trigger, exacerbate, or worsen depression in individuals with bipolar disorder. Specifically, a construct known in the psychology world as *expressed emotion (EE)* refers to a pattern of expression involving criticism, hostility, or emotional overinvolvement/ overprotectiveness.

Expressed emotion may include comments by family members or friends such as "You're lazy" or "Why can't you get your act together?" Expressed emotion can also be displayed by family members who are overly controlling or who try to make all the decisions.

Studies have shown that if people with bipolar disorder have a "caregiver" who expresses high levels of EE, they will be more likely to relapse or have more serious mood symptoms than individuals whose caregivers express low EE (Miklowitz and Johnson 2009). These types of relationship patterns appear to exacerbate a depressed mood more than they do an elevated one (Yan et al. 2004).

Substance Use

People with BPII have been shown to be at a higher risk of abusing alcohol and recreational drugs than the general population. Recreational drugs and excessive alcohol use can wreak havoc on your mood and clearly can contribute to depression. There is also some evidence that recreational drugs and alcohol may lower the efficacy of certain medications. Therefore, we strongly recommend that you abstain from recreational drugs and alcohol. If you do decide to drink alcohol, limit your intake, because alcohol can be a trigger for mood instability.

Identifying Your Triggers

Now that you have read about potential triggers for depression in people with BPII, we'd like you to take a few minutes to reflect on your previous or current episode(s) of depression and identify potential triggers of your depressive episodes.

Exercise 4.4.   Checklist: Your Triggers for Depression

Following is a list of some typical triggers for depression, but there are many other potential triggers. Place a check mark next to all that apply to you, and fill in additional triggers in the blank spaces provided.

_____ Loss of a job

_____ Loss of a relationship

_____ Death of a close friend or family member

_____ Increased stress at school or work

_____ My medical illness or injury

_____ Moving to a new place

_____ Having a baby

_____ Seasonal changes

_____ Graduating

_____ Alcohol or drug use

_____ Changes in sleep patterns

_____ Argument with a friend or family member

_____ Criticism from a family member

_____ Financial loss or setback

_____ A family members illness or medical issue

_____ Medication changes

_____ Menstrual cycle

_____ Traveling/vacation

_____ Getting married

_____ Failing a class

_____ Changing jobs

_____ Changes in daily routines

_____ _____

_____ _____

_____ _____

Monitoring Your Symptoms

One of the best ways to develop insight into or understanding of your symptoms is to track your mood on a daily basis. This will help you understand how daily stressors, changes in sleep patterns, and the effects of medications are all related to your mood. Ideally, it will also help you monitor and keep track of your medications on a daily basis, because you will check off the medications that you have taken.

Some online tools, such as those at Mood Tracker (moodtracker.com), can be very helpful in tracking your daily moods. You can also share these electronic mood charts with your care providers, which can help them monitor your mood as well. There are also some apps that enable you to track your mood using your smartphone.

Exercise 4.5.   Daily Diary Card

One of our clients with BPII came up with the following Daily Diary Card format and has used it for many years to track her mood, her life events, her medications, and the skills she uses to cope with her disorder. She has given her permission for us to share this form with you and hopes that it will help you understand and track your symptoms.

Following is a sample Daily Diary Card, as well as a blank one. An electronic version of this form can be found at http://www.newharbinger.com/27664 (see the back of this book for more information). We present the full Daily Diary Card here, but we do not expect you to fill out all the sections yet. Later in this book, we will cover topics related to mood elevation, anxiety, and skills to help you manage your BPII.

DAILY DIARY CARD (EXAMPLE)

Date: *4/9/14*

FEMALES ONLY: Did you have menstrual flow today? *No*

- What was the first day of your last period? *4/1/14*

Last night's SLEEP

- Time you went to bed last night: *10:00 p.m.*

- Time you woke up this morning: *8:00 a.m.*

Any naps today? *Yes. I took two naps and realize that I am sleeping too much.*

Did you sleep through the night? *Yes*

Did you have energy that sustained you throughout the day? *No, feeling tired*

ADDITIONAL NOTES ON SLEEP

I am going to bed at regularly scheduled time (10:00 p.m.) but having trouble getting up when alarm rings at 6:00 a.m.—oversleeping by two hours

MEDICATIONS TAKEN TODAY

1. _Lithium_ _____
2. _Wellbutrin_ _____
3. _____
4. _____
5. _____
6. _____
7. _____
8. _____

ADDITIONAL NOTES ON MEDICATIONS

Took both medications in the morning.

MOOD TRACKING (Check one)

_____ +3 SEVERELY ELEVATED (Significant Impairment; Not Able to Work)

_____ +2 MODERATELY ELEVATED (Significant Impairment; Able to Work)

_____ +1 MILDLY ELEVATED (No Significant Impairment; Able to Work)

_____ ±0 BASELINE ("Normal"/Grounded/Capable & Able/Productive)

_____ −1 MILDLY DEPRESSED (No Significant Impairment)

__√___ −2 MODERATELY DEPRESSED (Significant Impairment; Able to Work)

_____ −3 SEVERELY DEPRESSED (Significant Impairment; Not Able to Work)

Any thoughts of suicide today? _No_

Anxiety Rating*: *1*	COMMENTS: *Feeling mildly anxious today.*
Irritability Rating*: *2*	COMMENTS: *Feeling irritable and snapping at family members.*

* Rating: 0 = NONE, 1 = MILD, 2 = MODERATE, 3 = SEVERE

ADDITIONAL NOTES ON MOOD

Irritability was higher than it's been in several weeks.

Description of My Day

The day started with oversleeping and then scrambling to get to work on time. Missed my morning workout because of oversleeping. Feeling sluggish and lacking energy, even though I'm sleeping more than usual. Took a nap after work and then met friends for dinner. That was a positive part of my day, which I was tempted to cancel, but glad I followed through.

Skills I Used Today to Manage My Mood

I used relaxation exercises to manage my mild anxiety. I also scheduled and followed through with a pleasant activity (dinner with friends) even though I didn't feel like going.

DAILY DIARY CARD

Date: _____

FEMALES ONLY: Did you have menstrual flow today? _____

- What was the first day of your last period? _____

Last night's SLEEP

- Time you went to bed last night: _____

- Time you woke up this morning: _____

Any naps today? _____

_____

Did you sleep through the night? _____

_____

Did you have energy that sustained you throughout the day? _____

_____

ADDITIONAL NOTES ON SLEEP

_____

_____

MEDICATIONS TAKEN TODAY

1. _____

2. _____

3. _____

4. _____

5. _____

6. _____

7. _____

8. _____

ADDITIONAL NOTES ON MEDICATIONS

MOOD TRACKING (Check one)

_____ +3 SEVERELY ELEVATED (Significant Impairment; Not Able to Work)

_____ +2 MODERATELY ELEVATED (Significant Impairment; Able to Work)

_____ +1 MILDLY ELEVATED (No Significant Impairment; Able to Work)

_____ ±0 BASELINE ("Normal"/Grounded/Capable & Able/Productive)

_____ –1 MILDLY DEPRESSED (No Significant Impairment)

_____ –2 MODERATELY DEPRESSED (Significant Impairment; Able to Work)

_____ –3 SEVERELY DEPRESSED (Significant Impairment; Not Able to Work)

Any thoughts of suicide today? _____

Anxiety Rating*: _____	COMMENTS:
Irritability Rating*: _____	COMMENTS:

* Rating: 0 = NONE, 1 = MILD, 2 = MODERATE, 3 = SEVERE

ADDITIONAL NOTES ON MOOD

Description of My Day

Skills I Used Today to Manage My Mood

We will refer to this Daily Diary Card, or mood tracking system, throughout the book. In the next chapter, we will introduce skills for managing your depression, so don't worry if you didn't have anything to write under "Skills I Used Today to Manage My Mood." You will after you read the next chapter!

Chapter Summary:

- Depression is a frequent problem for people with BPII.

- Depression can be experienced in many different ways.

- It is important for you to understand the early signs, symptoms, and triggers of *your* depression.

- Suicide is a real risk for people with BPII, so you should have a plan in place to help you deal with suicidal thinking.

- Monitoring and tracking your depressive symptoms on a daily basis can help you understand your mood changes and sleep patterns and help you track your medication usage.

CHAPTER 5

Modifying Your Thinking and Behavior to Cope with Depression

In chapter 4, we discussed ways to recognize and understand your depression. Now, you are ready to take some action. In this chapter, we will teach you some powerful tools to help you tackle your depression.

How Your Thoughts, Mood, and Behaviors Are Related

Depression can have a profound effect on the way that people think and behave. When people are depressed, they tend to think about themselves, their world, and their future in an unrealistically negative way. Aaron T. Beck, the founder of cognitive therapy, was the first psychiatrist to recognize that depressed people have negative thinking styles that are often inaccurate or distorted (Beck 1976).

Imagine that you are looking through dark sunglasses at yourself, your world, and your future. Everything appears bleak, dark, and perhaps hopeless. You may be critical of your appearance, your abilities, or your relationships. You may think about your world or surroundings in an overly negative way. You may also see your future as hopeless or filled with dead ends. Now, imagine that you take off those dark sunglasses and see things in better light. Things might not be perfect, but your perspective is more accurate. If you've experienced depression in the past, you can likely relate to this example. When your depression lifted, you may have felt as if the dark lenses were removed.

The good news is that you do not need to wait for depression to lift in order to see things more clearly. The tools we will discuss in this chapter will help you examine your thoughts and take a more balanced perspective. Many research studies have shown that these strategies improve recovery from depression and can actually reduce the chances of relapse (Dobson 1989; Fava et al.

2004). We are not recommending that you wear rose-colored glasses, or view things in an unrealistically positive way. We will simply give you tools to view your situation more accurately. We will discuss strategies for healthier thinking that can help protect you from depression when you are faced with stressful life events. Later in this chapter, we will also discuss ways to change your behaviors to improve your mood.

Before we go further, it's important to explain that the way that you think about a situation or an event can dramatically influence your mood and behavior. Thoughts, feelings, and behaviors are tightly interrelated. When something stressful or uncertain happens, your thoughts can push you around. Negative thinking can actually increase your chances of becoming depressed or anxious in response to a stressful situation. So, there is a powerful relationship between thoughts, feelings or moods, and behaviors. As shown in the following figure, there is a cyclical relationship between thoughts, feelings, and behaviors, and they all have the capacity to affect one another.

Figure 5.1. Cyclical relationship of thoughts, feelings, and behaviors

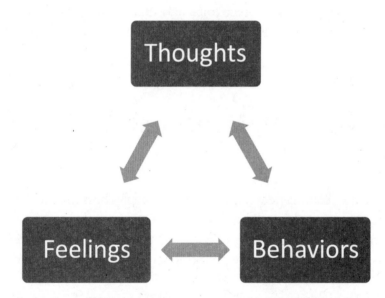

Let's take a look at how the same situation can have dramatically different outcomes depending on the interpretation or thoughts that a person has in response to it.

Taylor is a thirty-five-year-old graphic designer. She just started a new job a few weeks ago at an advertising firm. One morning, her boss indicates that he would like to meet with her in his office at the end of the day. Taylor can interpret this situation in a variety of different ways.

Figure 5.2. Two interpretations of Taylor's situation

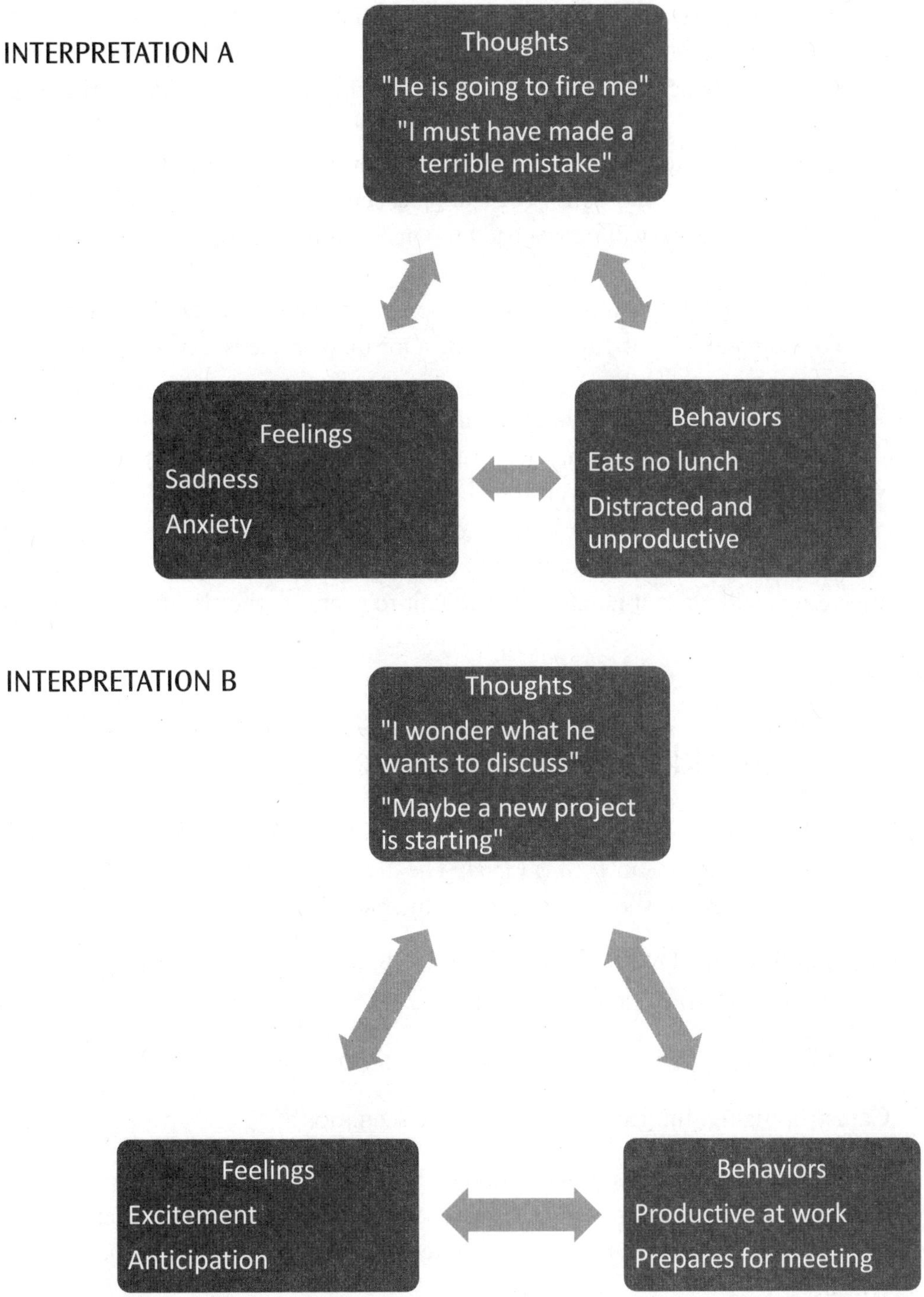

INTERPRETATION A

Thoughts
"He is going to fire me"
"I must have made a terrible mistake"

Feelings
Sadness
Anxiety

Behaviors
Eats no lunch
Distracted and unproductive

INTERPRETATION B

Thoughts
"I wonder what he wants to discuss"
"Maybe a new project is starting"

Feelings
Excitement
Anticipation

Behaviors
Productive at work
Prepares for meeting

As you can see, the exact same situation (i.e., Taylor's boss asking to meet with her) leads to completely different feelings and behaviors for her in interpretation A versus interpretation B. In fact, in interpretation A, Taylor's interpretation about the situation may actually bring about the outcome she feared, because she does less at work that day. This type of interpretation can be a self-fulfilling prophecy: your thoughts and fears actually can bring about the situation that you are most fearing.

In interpretation A, Taylor interprets the situation using several mistakes in thinking, or *cognitive errors* (also known as *cognitive distortions*). For example, she engages in negative *fortune telling*, convincing herself that the meeting will have a bad outcome or that her boss is judging her performance negatively.

She also engages in *catastrophizing* (imagining the worst-case scenario), another common type of cognitive error. For example, even if Taylor has made a mistake or needs feedback, her boss isn't necessarily going to fire her.

Have you ever jumped to a drastic conclusion, only to find out that you had misinterpreted the situation? Your feelings about the situation, though they may have been powerful, resulted from thoughts that weren't necessarily true or even based on facts. Engaging in thinking that is full of cognitive errors or distortions can make it much more likely that you will have strong negative emotions in response to potentially ambiguous or harmless situations. Even if a situation is truly negative, cognitive errors will make it much more difficult to examine the situation in a balanced way.

Exercise 5.1.   Checklist: Your Cognitive Distortions

Based on the work of psychiatrist Aaron Beck (1976), Dr. David Burns (1980, 1999) outlined many common cognitive distortions in *Feeling Good: The New Mood Therapy*. Read through the list and place a check mark next to the ones that sometimes show up in your thinking.

_____ **Fortune Telling:** Thinking that I "know" how a situation is going to turn out without having any evidence

_____ **Mind Reading:** Thinking that I "know" what someone else is thinking

_____ **Catastrophizing:** Imagining the worst-case scenario

_____ **All-or-Nothing Thinking** (also known as Black-and-White Thinking): Seeing things as either black or white, with no gray or middle ground; things are either wonderful or awful, with nothing in between; terms such as "always" or "never" are typical

_____ **Mental Filter:** Focusing on the negative details of an event or situation, without seeing the full picture

_____ **Personalizing:** Blaming myself as the sole cause of an event or situation

_____ **Jumping to Conclusions:** Reaching conclusions (usually negative) using only small amounts of evidence

_____ **Overgeneralizing:** Taking isolated incidents and making broad generalizations; seeing a single negative situation as a pattern of failure

_____ **Magnifying or Minimizing:** Making a big deal of the negatives and understating the positives

_____ **Discounting the Positives:** Similar to minimizing: receiving a compliment or praise and discounting it

_____ **Labeling:** Using negative self-talk, such as _I'm a loser_ or _I am an idiot_

_____ **Should-Statements:** Using rigid rules or statements, such as "I should be able to do this," rather than focusing on the actual situation

_____ **Emotional Reasoning:** Using emotions as truths; for example, "I feel like a loser; therefore, I must be a loser"

Developing Healthier Thinking Patterns

Now that you have learned about the concept of cognitive errors or distortions, how can you detect and modify these types of thinking styles in your everyday life?

The best way to notice your thinking patterns is to identify _automatic thoughts_. Automatic thoughts are thoughts that seem to arise on their own in response to events or situations. These automatic thoughts happen all the time, so they tend to "fly under the radar" of your awareness. Negative or unhealthy automatic thoughts typically contain some of the cognitive distortions listed in exercise 5.1.

The best way to tune in to your negative automatic thoughts is to pay close attention to your mood. When your mood suddenly worsens, simply ask yourself, _What thought just went through my mind?_ You might be amazed by how much "self-talk" you notice, once you train yourself to do this.

In table 5.1, there are some examples of automatic thoughts containing cognitive distortions. We also list the types of emotions/feelings and potential behaviors that might result from these automatic thoughts.

Table 5.1. Examples of Automatic Thoughts Containing Cognitive Distortions and Resulting Emotions and Behaviors

Situation	Automatic Thought	Cognitive Distortions	Emotions	Behaviors
Your girlfriend doesn't call when she's supposed to.	*She's going to break up with me.*	Catastrophizing, Jumping to Conclusions, Fortune Telling	sadness, fear	You cry and put away your pictures of her.
You don't get invited to a party.	*I am a loser.*	Labeling, Overgeneralizing, Emotional Reasoning	sadness, loneliness	You write the host an angry e-mail.
You receive a bad grade on one test.	*I am stupid and I will never get a good job.*	Catastrophizing, Labeling, Fortune Telling	fear, sadness, hopelessness	You stop studying or stop going to class.
You receive a compliment.	*She's only saying that to be nice.*	Mind Reading, Minimizing, Discounting the Positives	sadness, embarrassment, annoyance	You avoid eye contact.
Your friend doesn't wave back.	*He must be angry at me.*	Mind Reading, Personalizing	sadness, irritability, guilt	You decide that this person is no longer your friend.

As you can see, negative automatic thoughts can have a powerful effect on your mood and behaviors. The good news is that it is possible to change these negative automatic thoughts, in two basic steps.

Step 1: Record Your Automatic Thoughts and Emotions

The first step toward developing healthier thinking involves getting to know your automatic thoughts. Imagine that one afternoon at work, Judy experiences a negative shift in her mood. We will show you how to track automatic thoughts in a worksheet format, using Judy's situation.

Judy's Example Depressive Automatic Thought Record (Part 1)

Situation (Who/What/Where/When)

On Tuesday at 3:00 p.m., while we were at work, my friend Scott told me about a party that a mutual friend was having to which I had not been invited.

Automatic Thought

What was going through my mind just before I began to feel depressed? What does that mean about me? What does this mean about me in the big picture (my life and future)? What am I afraid might happen? What is the worst thing that could happen if this is true? What does this suggest in terms of what the other person might think or feel about me? Or, what does this mean about the other person or people in general?

I am a loser.

How much do I believe this automatic thought? (0–100%) *60%*

Cognitive Errors (Circle all that apply.)

Fortune Telling	Mind Reading	Catastrophizing
All-or-Nothing Thinking	Mental Filter	Personalizing
Jumping to Conclusions	(Overgeneralizing)	Magnifying or Minimizing
Discounting the Positives	(Labeling)	Should-Statements
(Emotional Reasoning)		

Emotion	**Strength** (1–100)
Sadness	*80*
Loneliness	*60*
Shame	*100*

As you can see, the first step Judy used to identify her automatic thoughts was to identify the situation that triggered her mood shift: the event or circumstance that led to or preceded the unpleasant emotion. She was very objective in explaining the situation, just noting the facts by answering the following questions about the situation: Who was I with? Where was I? What was I doing? When did it happen?

Keep in mind that a situation can be very simple, such as lying in bed or pouring a cup of coffee. Judy's situation was being at work and finding out from her friend Scott that another friend was having a party to which she was not invited.

Judy went over the list of questions in the next section to help her identify an automatic thought associated with her mood shift. Judy noted the first automatic thought that came to her mind: *I am a loser*. Then, she recorded how much she believed this automatic thought, from 0 to 100 percent. Finally, she identified from the list what types of cognitive errors may have been present. In this example, Judy likely made several cognitive errors, because not being invited to a party is not evidence that she is a loser. There could be many reasons why she was not invited—maybe the host wanted to keep the party small, maybe the host thought Judy would not be interested, or maybe the host is not a very nice person. But none of these possibilities supports the thought that Judy is a loser.

The final step in tracking automatic thoughts is understanding how they affect your emotions. This involves thinking carefully about how a specific automatic thought triggers emotions. For Judy, the thought of being a loser was associated with sadness, loneliness, and shame.

Using Judy's example as a guide, now practice identifying one of your own automatic thoughts in exercise 5.2. It can be helpful to first try to think of a recent mood shift—this will identify a situation that likely triggered some automatic thoughts.

Exercise 5.2.   Depressive Automatic Thought Record (Part 1)

Over the next few days, keep copies of the following form with you and fill it in whenever you notice a mood shift or change in your emotions for the worse. Try to capture a wide range of emotions, including sadness, fear, frustration, irritability, and guilt. You may identify many automatic thoughts in the same situation, each of which could be recorded on a separate Automatic Thought Record.

Situation (Who/What/Where/When)

_____

_____

Automatic Thought

What was going through my mind just before I began to feel depressed? What does that mean about me? What does this mean about me in the big picture (my life and future)? What am I afraid might happen? What is the worst thing that could happen if this is true? What does this suggest in terms of what the other person might think or feel about me? Or, what does this mean about the other person or people in general?

_____

How much do I believe this automatic thought? (0–100%) _____

Cognitive Errors (Circle all that apply.)

Fortune Telling	Mind Reading	Catastrophizing
All-or-Nothing Thinking	Mental Filter	Personalizing
Jumping to Conclusions	Overgeneralizing	Magnifying or Minimizing
Discounting the Positives	Labeling	Should-Statements
Emotional Reasoning		

Emotion   **Strength** (1–100)

_____   _____

_____   _____

_____   _____

Step 2: Modify Your Thinking

The next step in modifying your thinking, also known as *cognitive restructuring*, involves examining the evidence for your thoughts. Think of yourself as a scientist testing a hypothesis. In the beginning of this chapter, we talked about getting an accurate, not necessarily "rosy," perspective on your thoughts. By testing out your thinking, you are starting to take off the dark lenses of depression and see things more clearly.

The following questions will help you test out your thinking:

1. What is the objective evidence that my thought is true?

2. What are some alternatives that might help explain the situation?

3. If a friend were in this situation and had this thought, what would I tell him or her?

4. What is the effect of this thought on my mood? Are there any benefits? Are there any costs?

5. What's the worst that could happen if this thought is true? What's the best that could happen? What's the most realistic outcome?

These questions will help you examine your thoughts in a more objective way. Remember that your automatic thoughts are not necessarily "true," and emotions are not necessarily proof of anything, even if they feel very powerful.

In the second part of the Automatic Thought Record, you record your responses to the questions we just listed. You also rate the degree to which you believe these responses (0–100%), just as you did for your automatic thought in the first part. Then, you re-rate the degree to which you believe your initial automatic thought. You also re-rate the intensity of your emotions. Finally, you try to construct a more balanced or healthier thought, taking into account all the evidence that you have examined.

Judy's Example Depressive Automatic Thought Record (Parts 1 and 2)

Part 1

Situation (Who/What/Where/When)

On Tuesday at 3:00 p.m., while we were at work, my friend Scott told me about a party that a mutual friend was having to which I had not been invited.

Automatic Thought

What was going through my mind just before I began to feel depressed? What does that mean about me? What does this mean about me in the big picture (my life and future)? What am I afraid might happen? What is the worst thing that could happen if this is true? What does this suggest in terms of what the other person might think or feel about me? Or, what does this mean about the other person or people in general?

I am a loser.

How much do I believe this automatic thought? (0–100%) 60%

Cognitive Errors (Circle all that apply.)

Fortune Telling	Mind Reading	Catastrophizing
All-or-Nothing Thinking	Mental Filter	Personalizing
Jumping to Conclusions	⟨Overgeneralizing⟩	Magnifying or Minimizing
Discounting the Positives	⟨Labeling⟩	Should-Statements
⟨Emotional Reasoning⟩		

Emotion	Strength (1–100)
Sadness	*80*
Loneliness	*60*
Shame	*100*

Part 2

What is the objective evidence that my thought is true?

There is really no evidence that I am a loser. (90%) I have many other friends and often get invited to other parties. (100%)

What are some alternatives that might help explain the situation?

The reality is that I do not know the host of the party all that well, even though we have some mutual friends. (100%) The host may have had space constraints which limited the guest list. (60%)

If a friend were in this situation and had this thought, what would I tell him or her?

I would tell a friend not to worry about it because your friends still care about you and it does not make you a loser. (100%)

What is the effect of this thought on my mood? Are there any benefits? Are there any costs?

This thought has a really bad impact on my mood and does not help me at all. (100%)

What's the worst that could happen if this thought is true? What's the best that could happen? What's the most realistic outcome?

There really is no worst-case scenario. (80%) Best-case scenario is that I find something more fun to do that night. (70%)

How much do I believe this automatic thought now? (0–100%) *10%*

Emotion	Strength (1–100)
Sadness	*10*
Loneliness	*10*
Shame	*10*

Balanced or Healthier Thought

Even though it is disappointing to feel left out, I still have many other friends and I am not a loser. (90%)

Exercise 5.3.   Depressive Automatic Thought Record (Parts 1 and 2)

Now, it's your turn to use one of your Automatic Thought Records, part 1, and practice responding to your automatic thoughts. Remember, an electronic version of the Automatic Thought Record is available at http://www.newharbinger.com/27664 (see the back of this book for more information).

Part 1

Situation (Who/What/Where/When)

_____

_____

Automatic Thought

What was going through my mind just before I began to feel depressed? What does that mean about me? What does this mean about me in the big picture (my life and future)? What am I afraid might happen? What is the worst thing that could happen if this is true? What does this suggest in terms of what the other person might think or feel about me? Or, what does this mean about the other person or people in general?

_____

How much do I believe this automatic thought? (0–100%) _____

Cognitive Errors (Circle all that apply.)

Fortune Telling	Mind Reading	Catastrophizing
All-or-Nothing Thinking	Mental Filter	Personalizing
Jumping to Conclusions	Overgeneralizing	Magnifying or Minimizing
Discounting the Positives	Labeling	Should-Statements
Emotional Reasoning		

Emotion **Strength** (1–100)

_____ _____

_____ _____

_____ _____

Part 2

What is the objective evidence that my thought is true?

_____

_____

What are some alternatives that might help explain the situation?

_____

_____

If a friend were in this situation and had this thought, what would I tell him or her?

_____

_____

What is the effect of this thought on my mood? Are there any benefits? Are there any costs?

_____

_____

What's the worst that could happen if this thought is true? What's the best that could happen? What's the most realistic outcome?

_____

_____

How much do I believe this automatic thought now? (0–100%) _____

Emotion	Strength (1–100)
_____	_____
_____	_____
_____	_____

Balanced or Healthier Thought

_____

_____

In summary, your goal in using the Depressive Automatic Thought Record is to systematically question and evaluate your negative automatic thoughts and to construct a more realistic and balanced response to the event or situation—in other words, to take off the dark sunglasses. The goal is not to avoid or eliminate distressing situations or thoughts, but instead to equip yourself with tools to respond to them more effectively.

Bipolar II disorder (BPII) will inevitably cause mood shifts, which will result in automatic thoughts becoming more negative at times. However, you can take action by examining your thoughts, or noticing the way you talk to yourself, and realizing that these thoughts, no matter how powerful their associated emotions, are not necessarily true just because you have thought them. As a reminder, everyone makes cognitive errors (which is why we have names for them!), but you are more prone to making them given that you have BPII. Thus, you need to regularly practice the skill of monitoring and changing your thinking, known as cognitive restructuring, to help you solve your problems or face difficult situations more effectively.

Developing Healthier Behaviors

So far in this chapter, we discussed the complex interplay between thoughts, emotions, and behaviors, but we have focused primarily on ways that you can detect and modify your negative thinking. Now, we turn our focus toward modifying your behaviors to help with your depression, which is referred to as *behavioral activation*.

Have you ever felt so depressed that the idea of getting out of bed was overwhelming? Have everyday tasks, such as loading the dishwasher or taking a shower, seemed impossible?

When your depression is severe and your energy levels are low, it may feel more manageable to first target behaviors, rather than thoughts. Setting small goals, such as getting dressed or walking the dog, can be helpful in activating or improving your mood.

Exercise 5.4.   Checklist: Behavioral Goals

Place a check mark next to the everyday tasks that you find challenging when you are depressed. In the blank spaces, fill in other tasks that apply.

_____	Waking up	_____	Getting out of bed
_____	Showering	_____	Getting dressed
_____	Cooking	_____	Walking the dog
_____	Doing dishes	_____	Doing laundry
_____	Grocery shopping	_____	Brushing my teeth
_____	Keeping my planned activities	_____	Opening mail
_____	Taking out garbage	_____	Paying bills
_____	Taking care of kids	_____	Getting to work
_____	Talking on the phone	_____	Responding to messages/e-mails
_____	Taking medications	_____	Getting to bed on time
_____	Exercising	_____	Calling a friend
_____	_____	_____	_____
_____	_____	_____	_____

So, how can you tackle activities that seem impossible when you are very depressed? The following steps can help:

- Set small, manageable goals. On a really bad day, your goal might be to simply get out of bed and get dressed. Once you are dressed, you might find that you have the energy to get some other tasks accomplished.

- Set time limits for difficult tasks. For example, if you have a pile of dishes in the sink, it might be overwhelming to think about getting all of them clean. Make a deal with yourself to spend only five minutes doing dishes. Similarly, if you have a pile of mail to open and you are dreading this task, commit to working on it for five-minute intervals. Set a timer.

- Try to have empathy or understanding for yourself. Don't hold yourself to the same standards as when you are feeling well. Take each day and small step at a time.

- Remember that "depression hates activity!" The more you can push yourself to be active, the less likely it is that you will become or stay depressed.

- Exercise can have a powerful effect on your mood. Even short bursts of activity can be highly effective. If you are having a really hard day, pushing yourself to get outside for even a five-minute walk can make you feel better. (We will talk more about exercise in chapter 6.)

Choosing Your Activities

Not all behaviors are equal. Some behaviors or activities can be helpful in giving you a sense of accomplishment, such as paying bills or doing laundry. Other activities or behaviors can be associated with feelings of pleasure or enjoyment, such as meeting friends for dinner or going to the movies. For many people, the best types of activities involve some degree of enjoyment and accomplishment. For example, organizing photos from a vacation might give you both a sense of accomplishment and pleasure. Playing a sport or training for a race might be both fun and productive.

Think about how you spend your time when you are depressed. It is not uncommon for people with depression to engage in activities that rate low in both pleasure and accomplishment. Lying in bed or watching hours of television might be such an activity.

Exercise 5.5.   Identifying Pleasurable and Productive Activities

In the following table, write down a few types of activities that you associate with pleasure, a few that you associate with accomplishment or productiveness, and ideally a few that you associate with both. If you're stumped, think about activities that lead to pleasure or productivity when you are feeling well. You may also find it useful to ask a family member or friend to help you brainstorm these types of activities. Finally, list some of the activities that you engage in when you are depressed that are low in both accomplishment or productivity and pleasure. We have included a few examples to get you started.

Pleasurable Activities	Productive Activities	Activities That Are Both Pleasurable and Productive	Activities That Are Neither Pleasurable nor Productive
Having a favorite meal	Paying bills	Gardening	Lying on my couch
Getting a manicure	Cleaning dishes	Taking my kids to the zoo	Watching TV

Loss of interest is a major symptom of depression, and it is likely that you will not feel like doing pleasurable or productive activities when you are depressed. You may also derive less enjoyment or feelings of accomplishment from them. However, it is important that you push yourself to do these things. You have probably heard the old saying "Practice makes perfect." Well, it applies here, because you will get better at enjoying pleasurable things each time you try. Take small steps. Remember that engaging in positive behaviors (even when you don't feel like it) is likely to improve both your mood and your thoughts and, at the very least, is highly unlikely to make your mood worse! Don't give up, even if it's tough. Activity is always better than inactivity.

Keeping a Regular Schedule

Did you know that the regularity of your daily routines, otherwise known as *social rhythms*, can help stabilize your mood? Your daily routine may be waking up, having breakfast, showering, and going to work; or it may be waking up, walking your dog, and going to the coffee shop. No matter what your particular social rhythm is, people with bipolar disorder can benefit greatly from adopting a predictable pattern of activities (Frank et al. 2005).

However, as discussed in chapter 2, people with BPII may have especial difficulty maintaining structure in their daily social rhythms. Furthermore, a lack of structure can contribute to episodes of depression or hypomania. Therefore, in this section we focus on important strategies and tools for structuring your schedule to help prevent mood episodes. Let us begin by discussing one of the most important social rhythms for individuals with BPII: sleep.

SLEEPING

Sleep loss or irregular sleep patterns (such as sometimes sleeping excessively or napping) can destabilize your mood. In general, you should adopt a regular sleeping schedule on both weekdays and weekends. Try to avoid staying up late to meet work deadlines or cram for exams. If possible, work the same shift (e.g., day, evening, or graveyard) all the time, because rotating your sleep/wake cycle can have serious consequences on your mood. Traveling across time zones may be problematic, and gradual adjustment to a new time zone may be beneficial in minimizing the effects on your mood. For example, if you will be traveling from New York to California, you can gradually go to bed later and wake up later in the days leading up to your trip.

Researchers have found that many people with BPII have elevated energy in the evenings, which can lead to staying up later than planned. Try to maintain discipline with regard to winding down your evening activities and maintaining a set bedtime. Remember to turn off your computer or television at least thirty minutes prior to your scheduled bedtime. It's also important to avoid oversleeping or excessive napping when you are depressed. Overall, shoot for the same, structured sleep schedule regardless of your mood.

Of course, this is easier said than done. Stressful life events may interfere with your regular routines. Insomnia (sleeping too little) or hypersomnia (sleeping too much) can also be a symptom of depression. Ask your doctor about medications that may help you maintain a regular sleep schedule. However, beyond medications, the cognitive skills discussed earlier in this chapter can also help you change any negative thoughts about your sleep, such as *I will never get to sleep* or *I can't get out of bed*. Mindfulness meditation and relaxation exercises (as discussed in chapters 6 and 10) may also help prepare you for sleep.

EATING

Not only are regular, predictable mealtimes good for your metabolism and overall health, but they can also help your mood. We will discuss the importance of eating well in chapter 6, but for now, you should focus on tracking your mealtimes and trying to maintain structured eating habits. Meals are an important part of establishing a good, daily social rhythm.

MEDICATION USE

Take your medications at regularly scheduled times. Include this as a scheduled part of your daily routine.

EXERCISE

The benefits of physical activity for your mood will be discussed further in chapter 6, but exercise can also be an important way to structure your day. Thus, you should schedule regular times to exercise.

WORK

A regular work schedule may not be feasible for all people. However, we highly recommend that you avoid rotating shift work, if possible. A regular, predictable daily schedule is preferable for stabilizing your mood.

SOCIAL INTERACTION

Ideally, you should schedule regular times for social interaction. If you share a roof (e.g., with family or roommates), social interaction might be a natural part of your day. If you live alone, try to schedule weekly times to share a meal with a friend or interact with others in a social setting. Interacting with others improves your social skills, which is important for keeping jobs, having good relations with family, and meeting new people. Joining an exercise class, taking a pottery course, or joining a support group are other ways to increase your social interaction.

Exercise 5.6.   Scheduling Daily Activities

Use the following table to establish target times for daily activities and to keep track of the timing of these activities over the coming week. Try to maintain consistency by keeping within forty-five minutes of the target time for each activity. For example, if you make your target wake-up time 9:00 a.m. (as in the example), then you will have met this goal if you wake up between 8:15 and 9:45 a.m. Therefore, if you woke up at 9:30 on Monday and 8:30 on Wednesday, you can check the boxes for these days because you will have met your goal.

Activity	Target Time	Mon	Tue	Wed	Thu	Fri	Sat	Sun
Example: *Wake up*	9:00 a.m.	9:30 a.m. √	10:00 a.m.	8:30 a.m. √	11:15 a.m.	10:30 a.m.	11:00 a.m.	*Noon*
Breakfast								
Morning medication								
Work								
Lunch								
Exercise								
Social interaction								
Dinner								
Evening medication								
Bedtime								
Other:								
Other:								

At the end of the week, review the table. If you didn't meet your goals, do some reflection to identify what interfered with regularity in your routines. For example, did you get caught up watching TV and have difficulty getting to bed on time? Were you in a rush to get to work, causing you to postpone or skip breakfast? Perhaps you intended to exercise, but did not follow through on getting to the gym. Developing a regular daily routine can be challenging, and it can take some time to master. Exercise 5.7 will help you overcome obstacles to maintaining a regular schedule.

Exercise 5.7.   Problem Solving About Daily Routines

It can be particularly helpful to complete this exercise with your partner, a family member, or another person who knows your routine well. Ask yourself the following questions, and write your answers in the spaces below.

What interfered with sticking to my daily schedule? Why?

_____

_____

_____

_____

Which activities were most difficult? Why?

_____

_____

_____

_____

What can I do to minimize obstacles that interfere with regulating my schedule?

_____

_____

_____

Using These Skills to Cope with Depression and Prevent Relapse

In this chapter, we have discussed the importance of using tools to tackle your depression. Many of these strategies can also be preventive. If you start to feel the downward spiral of depression, you can use these tools to prevent a full episode from occurring. Reflect on how you experience mild, moderate, and severe levels of depression, and think about how you can use these tools at each stage.

For example, using Automatic Thought Records to identify and modify cognitive distortions can be helpful in minimizing the impact of stressful situations. In addition, it can decrease the likelihood that you will become depressed in response to difficult events, because you can restructure your distorted, negative thinking before it significantly affects your mood.

Behavioral tools, such as keeping a regular schedule and engaging in pleasurable and productive activities, are helpful strategies in preventing depressive episodes. Ideally, you should be using these tools every day. In the context of a severe depressive episode, setting small behavioral goals, such as showering or taking a five-minute walk, can help activate your mood and clear your thoughts. When you are depressed, you may need to work extra hard to keep your sleep cycle consistent—for example, using medications to help you sleep, or forcing yourself to get out of bed. This is also an important time to seek help or support from others.

The last exercise of this chapter, exercise 5.8, is designed to help you identify which skills may be most helpful and when (i.e., for mild versus moderate versus severe depression). This exercise will be very helpful when you create your Personalized Wellness Plan in chapter 12, so take some time to do it now, while the strategies we discussed in this chapter are still fresh in your mind.

Exercise 5.8.   Tools for Coping with Depression and Preventing Relapse

In this exercise, you will begin to make a plan to prevent depressive episodes by thinking about which strategies will help you at what times.

First, think about how you experience various stages of depression. What are the earliest symptoms you experience, also known as *early warning signs*? How can you tell that an episode is brewing? When you are a bit deeper into a depressive episode, what types of symptoms or problems arise? Finally, when you are severely depressed, what symptoms are most difficult for you?

Then, think about the tools discussed in this chapter and how you can use them to intervene at each stage of depression. For example, when might it be most helpful for you to practice cognitive restructuring (i.e., changing your thinking), and when might it be most helpful to focus on changing your behaviors (i.e., by adding pleasurable activities to your daily schedule)? Ideally, you will routinely use both cognitive and behavioral strategies, but it may become more difficult to challenge your thinking as you become more depressed, and, therefore, you may find that behavioral skills are best during these times.

Finally, fill in the blanks, looking back over the chapter if you need to.

Coping with Depression

When I am in the *mild or early* stages of depression, I experience the following symptoms:

_____

_____

_____

_____

Tools I can use to help myself during this time:

_____

_____

_____

_____

When I feel *moderately* depressed, I experience the following symptoms:

_____

_____

_____

_____

Tools I can use to help myself during this time:

_____

_____

_____

_____

When I am *severely* depressed, I experience the following symptoms:

_____

_____

_____

_____

Tools I can use to help myself during this time:

_____

_____

_____

_____

Preventing Relapse

Tools I can use every day to stay well:

_____

_____

_____

_____

Chapter Summary:

- Thoughts, feelings, and behaviors are tightly interrelated.

- Modifying your thinking and your behavior can help you feel better.

- Thoughts are not always accurate or true, even if they feel very powerful.

- Automatic Thought Records can help you identify and modify distorted thoughts.

- Setting small behavioral goals can help you improve your mood.

- Regulating your daily routines can improve your mood and prevent depressive episodes.

- You have the power to improve your depression by using these tools.

CHAPTER 6

More Strategies for Modifying Your Thoughts and Behavior

Many people with bipolar II disorder (BPII) feel overwhelmed at times by their negative emotions or impulses. In these situations, it may seem as though the pain will never end. It can be hard to think clearly; and using coping techniques, like the cognitive restructuring skills discussed in chapter 5, may seem very difficult. As a result, some people resort to using unhealthy coping behaviors. This chapter builds upon chapter 5 to provide you with additional strategies for coping with your depressed mood in healthy ways. In particular, these skills should prove useful when you feel overwhelmed by your negative emotions. These strategies are different from those discussed in chapter 5; they focus on how to tolerate, or just "sit with," uncomfortable emotions, as opposed to trying to change them. The first set of strategies we discuss in this chapter, called distress tolerance skills (Linehan 1993b), seek not to change your negative thoughts, but rather to distract you from them. We will also introduce mindfulness, which is a skill that can help you focus on one thing at a time so that you can better control your emotions. The last part of this chapter discusses good nutrition and exercise habits, both of which can contribute to better physical health as well as improved mood.

Dealing with Overwhelming Emotions and Urges

Have you ever had an emotional crisis? During such times, your emotions about a particular situation are so strong that they feel overwhelming. For example, if you are in the midst of a depressive episode and get into a serious argument with your partner or spouse, you may start to believe that your depression is never going to improve and that your relationship cannot be salvaged. You may think that you are out of control, helpless, and hopeless, and you may wonder how you can cope in that moment. Afterward you may find yourself thinking a lot about the argument and blaming yourself for the things you said and did and, perhaps, getting even more upset the more that you think about it.

It is common for people with BPII to go through periods of feeling overwhelmed by their negative emotions. These periods can occur during a mood episode, but they can also occur outside of an episode. When people feel this way, they often have urges or impulses to engage in unhealthy coping strategies. For example, you may want to drink lots of alcohol, overeat, or hurt yourself in some other way as a method of managing these overwhelming emotions. Although engaging in these behaviors may make you feel good for a short time, they can have negative consequences in the long run. For example, continued alcohol use can lead to poor decision making, problems with family or friends, and negative health consequences.

Exercise 6.1. Consequences of Unhealthy Coping Strategies

Take some time to think about unhealthy ways in which you have coped with overwhelming negative emotions in the past. In the following table are several unhealthy coping strategies. Place a check mark next to the behaviors that apply to you, and indicate the short-term as well as long-term consequences of the behavior. We have left space for you to write in other unhealthy behaviors that you might engage in.

Unhealthy Coping Behavior	(√)	Short-Term Consequence	Long-Term Consequence
Example: *Using drugs*	√	*It made me forget about why I was sad.*	*I started using them so much that it became difficult to keep my friends and go to my job.*
Using drugs			
Using alcohol			
Binge eating			

Smoking cigarettes			
Purging			
Isolating			
Cutting/hurting myself			
Yelling at others			
Threatening to hurt myself			
Putting myself in dangerous situations (e.g., risky sex/driving)			
Oversleeping			

As we discussed, many people with BPII feel overwhelmed at times by their negative emotions or impulses. When you are feeling overwhelmed, it may be difficult to think clearly and engage in healthy coping techniques, such as the cognitive restructuring skills discussed in chapter 5. The next set of skills, called *distress tolerance skills*, tend to require less cognitive effort (i.e., thinking power) and, therefore, can be particularly useful when you feel overwhelmed. Distress tolerance skills were developed as part of a psychotherapy called dialectical behavior therapy (DBT; see chapter 2) (Linehan 1993a, b). DBT skills, such as distress tolerance skills, can be very helpful to people trying to manage overwhelming feelings and avoid engaging in unhealthy coping strategies. Distress tolerance skills are not designed to make your emotions disappear or to solve the situation that is making you feel overwhelmed. Instead, they help you tolerate your strong emotions so that you do not engage in unhealthy coping strategies or make the situation worse (Linehan 1993b).

The distress tolerance skills that we discuss in this chapter are called *distracting skills* (Linehan 1993b). These skills are designed to distract you from unpleasant or painful thoughts or memories and keep you from engaging in unhealthy coping strategies.

Distraction Through Engaging in an Activity

Distracting yourself from painful thoughts and feelings can be an effective way to manage overwhelming situations. Distraction techniques provide temporary relief. The goal of distraction is to reduce strong emotions so that you can eventually go back to the overwhelming situation to process and deal with it (Linehan 1993b). This goal of returning to the situation is important, because it is the difference between distraction and *avoidance*. Avoidance is when you have no plan to process or deal with the situation, or try to forget or deny that the situation ever happened.

Exercise 6.2.   Checklist: Distracting Activities

Here are a number of activities that may help distract you from overwhelming emotions. Not all of them will appeal to you, and that is okay. You can use the spaces at the bottom of the list to write in other possible distracting activities. We suggest that you identify five to ten activities that seem as though they would be helpful, then write them down some place where you can refer to them easily, such as in your smartphone or on an index card that you keep in your wallet.

_____	Go for a walk or run.	_____	Take an exercise class at the gym.
_____	Watch old home movies.	_____	Play with modeling clay.
_____	Look at old photographs.	_____	Write e-mails to old friends.

_____	Walk to the nearest coffee shop.	_____	Listen to music.
_____	Meet a friend for lunch.	_____	Research my next vacation.
_____	Watch a funny TV program.	_____	Get a manicure, or paint my nails.
_____	Find and cook a new recipe.	_____	Do a crossword puzzle.
_____	Call an old friend.	_____	Take a hot shower.
_____	Get a massage.	_____	Visit a pet store.
_____	Learn to knit or crochet.	_____	Go to a museum.
_____	Take an adult education course.	_____	Join a volunteer organization.
_____	Snuggle into my bed.	_____	Sunbathe.
_____	Paint or draw.	_____	Go window shopping.
_____	Read a magazine.	_____	Find a good book.
_____	Go to the movies.	_____	_____
_____	_____	_____	_____
_____	_____		

Distraction Through Sensations

Another way to distract yourself from intense emotions and impulses is to use physical sensations (Linehan 1993b), such as your sense of touch, taste, sound, or smell. You can use either pleasant or unpleasant sensations to distract yourself. An example of a pleasant physical sensation is basking in the sun on a warm summer's day, and an example of an unpleasant sensation is holding a piece of ice in your hand. The type of sensation you use as a distraction may depend on your type of impulse. For example, if you are experiencing an urge to cut yourself, it may be more helpful to replace that urge with an unpleasant sensation, such as putting your hand in a bucket of ice-cold water, since that more closely resembles your urge than a pleasant sensation.

Exercise 6.3.   Checklist: Distracting Physical Sensations

Here are several ways to distract yourself by engaging your senses. Place a check mark next to those that may be particularly useful for you, and write in any others you can think of at the bottom.

Pleasant

_____ Sunbathing

_____ Taking a hot shower

_____ Getting a massage

_____ Boiling cinnamon (for fragrance)

_____ Burning a scented candle

_____ Going for a walk or drive

_____ Visiting a favorite location

_____ Savoring a special food

_____ _____

_____ _____

Unpleasant

_____ Pinching my forearm

_____ Going outside on a cold day in only a t-shirt

_____ Taking a cold shower

_____ Grasping a cold orange

_____ Snapping a rubber band on my wrist

_____ Sucking on a very strong mint

_____ Standing on one foot

_____ Holding a piece of ice

_____ _____

_____ _____

Distraction Through Coping Statements

You may find it helpful to distract yourself from overwhelming emotions and urges by using coping statements (McKay, Davis, and Fanning 1997). Coping statements can be thought of as encouraging and positive thoughts. Some examples are listed in the following exercise, but we encourage you to generate your own statements as well.

Exercise 6.4.   Checklist: Distracting Coping Statements

Pick several coping statements that you like from the following list, or write your own in the spaces at the bottom. Record them in your smartphone or on an index card that you will keep in your wallet for easy reference.

_____ This too shall pass.

_____ I have gotten through difficult situations in the past, and I can do it again.

_____ I am stronger than this situation.

_____ I won't let this get the better of me.

_____ This pain is only temporary.

_____ One step at a time; I can handle this situation.

_____ I can meet this challenge.

_____ This is not the worst thing that could happen.

_____ I tend to handle things better than I think I will.

_____ _____

_____ _____

_____ _____

If you found these skills helpful, you can read more about distracting activities, as well as other DBT skills, by referring to the "Further Reading" section at the end of this book.

Mindfulness

As you learned in chapter 5, your thoughts are a very powerful influence on your mood. The more negative thoughts you have, the more likely you will become depressed and the more likely your depressed mood will stick around. Many people who suffer from depression begin to judge themselves negatively for having a sad mood. So in addition to having sad thoughts, they then begin to have negative thoughts about their depressed mood and their ability to cope with it. This self-critical way of thinking is known as _rumination_. Rumination is the tendency to focus on the causes, meanings, and consequences of a depressed mood. Examples of ruminative thoughts are as follows:

- _Why do I always have to feel so sad?_

- _Why can't I deal with things better?_

- _What have I done to deserve this?_

You can probably see how this type of thinking would make a depressed mood even worse, and indeed research has shown that people who ruminate tend to have longer and more severe depressive episodes (Nolen-Hoeksema and Morrow 1991). So what is an alternative to rumination? It's called *mindfulness*.

Mindfulness can be described as "paying attention in a particular way: on purpose, in the present moment, and nonjudgmentally" (Kabat-Zinn 1994, 4). It is considered a core skill in DBT (Linehan 1993a). The term "mindfulness" has its roots in Eastern spiritual practices (Kabat-Zinn 1990), but you need not be religious to benefit from it. Indeed, the field of psychology has come to recognize that mindfulness can improve both physical and emotional well-being. As discussed in chapter 2, the skill of mindfulness has been used specifically as part of mindfulness-based cognitive therapy (MBCT) to address recurrent depressive episodes (Segal, Williams, and Teasdale 2002).

Mindfulness is about tuning in to what is going on in the present moment in your internal and external world, with openness, nonjudgment, and acceptance (which we introduced in chapter 3). Several studies have demonstrated that mindfulness can improve symptoms associated with bipolar disorder (Deckersbach et al. 2012; Perich et al. 2013), depression (Teasdale et al. 2000), and generalized anxiety disorder (Miller, Fletcher, and Kabat-Zinn 1995; Kutz, Borysenko, and Benson 1985).

So how is mindfulness different from rumination, or the repetitive, judgmental thinking that people often become stuck in? Williams et al. (2007) describe three ways in which mindfulness can be viewed as the opposite of rumination: first, mindfulness is intentional and purposeful, while rumination is automatic (and thus, not intentional) and serves no good purpose for people's ability to function or live. Second, mindfulness focuses directly on the present moment, while rumination consists of rehashing the past and rehearsing the future. Third, mindfulness is nonjudgmental and allows things to be viewed and accepted just as they are, while ruminative thinking is, by definition, judgmental.

The notion of *awareness* is a key element to practicing mindfulness. Awareness is crucial for three reasons. First, it is essential to be aware of your current negative thoughts, feelings, behaviors, and sensations, because this helps ground you in the present moment. Second, awareness and focus on the present moment can replace ruminative thoughts. Finally, awareness allows you to deliberately turn away from your negative, distorted thoughts, because it gives you a choice to focus on something else. Awareness of the present moment, or being mindful of the present moment, will help you disengage from negative thoughts. In doing so, you are taking control of your thoughts and taking charge of your mental state.

The following exercise is commonly used to introduce people to the concept of mindfulness. It teaches you how to start paying attention in a purposeful, nonjudgmental way, and it demonstrates a new way of relating to experiences that is at the heart of mindfulness.

Exercise 6.5.   Mindfully Observing an Everyday Object

One of the simplest ways to learn and practice mindfulness is through focusing on an everyday object. Typically, people pay little attention to everyday objects, so learning to focus your attention on such items is a good way to learn to observe things in a new way—the mindful way. For this exercise, choose an object that is edible so that you can observe it with all your five senses: touch, sight, sound, smell, and taste. It might be a piece of dry cereal, a strawberry, or a small piece of candy. Note: Throughout this exercise, your mind may wander to unrelated thoughts and feelings. When it does, gently bring your attention back to the object.

1. Hold the object in the palm of your hand, and look at it closely. Pretend that you've never seen it before. Describe out loud what you see, without judging it. Is it shiny? Is it smooth? Is the object all one color, or are there different colors on different surfaces of the object? Is it dark or light?

2. Hold the object between your fingers and gently squeeze it. Is it hard? Is it soft? Is it heavy? Light? Now run your fingers along the front and back of the object. It may help to close your eyes so that you can focus on how the object feels in your hand and between your fingers.

3. Gently shake the object and listen. Does it make a noise?

4. Lift the object to your nose and smell it. Again, it might be helpful to close your eyes. Does it smell sweet? Salty? Fresh? Stale?

5. Bring the object to your mouth. Run it gently along your lips so that you can start to taste it. Now put it in your mouth and hold it there for ten to fifteen seconds, without chewing or swallowing it. Explore its taste and texture with your tongue. How does it taste? How does it feel in your mouth? Now gently bite down on the object, paying close attention to how the taste changes. Chew slowly, and when you swallow, focus on how it feels as the object goes down your throat and into your stomach.

In chapter 5, you learned one of the key elements of cognitive behavioral therapy: how to recognize your negative, distorted thoughts and identify more realistic thoughts. In other words, you learned to change the content of your thoughts. However, sometimes changing unwanted thoughts, feelings, and body sensations is very difficult to do. Mindfulness takes a different approach to negative thoughts. The only goal in mindfulness is to be more aware of the present moment. Instead of seeking to change the content of your thoughts, mindfulness encourages you to accept your thoughts the way that they are, even if they are painful (you can read more about acceptance in chapter 3). Mindfulness seeks to change your *relationship* or *perspective* to your negative thoughts, feelings, and bodily sensations and encourages you to see them as simply passing events in your mind that are not necessarily valid or permanent.

There may be situations and times when the thought-changing strategies you learned in chapter 5 are most helpful, and there may be other situations and times when a mindful approach is more helpful. You will have to practice the different techniques in a variety of situations to see what works best for you and when.

If you are like some of our clients with BPII, it may not be immediately apparent how mindfulness may be helpful to you. Let us briefly discuss some different ways mindfulness can be helpful (Van Dijk 2009). Then we will illustrate them using Joaquin's story.

Emotion Awareness

Mindfulness helps you focus on the present moment, which means that when you are mindful you are more likely to recognize unhealthy emotions that could snowball into a depressive episode. Therefore, being mindful can help you avoid relapse because you will notice symptoms early, and you'll be able to take appropriate steps before those symptoms intensify.

Reducing Unhealthy Coping Strategies

When you are unaware of how you are thinking or feeling, you are more likely to engage in the unhealthy coping strategies that we discussed at the beginning of this chapter (drinking alcohol, overeating, self-harming, etc.). Mindfulness helps you be more aware of what you are thinking, doing, and feeling so that you can *choose* how you want to react, rather than automatically react in an unhealthy way. Thus, mindfulness gives you more control over your urges and actions.

Better Control of Your Thoughts

Mindfulness involves consciously directing your awareness. In this way, it allows you to gain control of your thoughts rather than have your thoughts control you. Therefore, mindfulness can reduce rumination and the painful emotions that arise from dwelling too much on the past or future.

Improvement in Memory and Concentration

One common symptom of depression is concentration difficulties, which can lead to memory problems. However, when you use mindfulness, you are fully engaged in whatever you are doing. Consequently, your concentration is focused, and you will be more likely to remember details of the activity.

More Positive Emotions

Much of people's emotional pain comes from thinking about the past and anticipating the future. It is very difficult to have more than one thought at the same time, so being mindful of the present moment prevents you from focusing on either the past or the future. It can also help you get the most out of the moment you are in. For example, if you are at a party but you are thinking about a painful breakup, it will likely be more difficult to enjoy the party. But if you can focus solely on the delicious food, interesting conversation, and enjoyable music at the party, you are more likely to experience positive emotions.

Relaxation

Although mindfulness is not necessarily intended to induce feelings of relaxation, this can sometimes be a pleasant by-product.

• Joaquin

Joaquin, twenty-six and single, is an English teacher and was diagnosed with BPII one year ago. Although he has been developing a better understanding of his symptoms and coping mechanisms, he still has much to learn. He starts practicing mindfulness at the suggestion of his therapist. Typically, he devotes about fifteen minutes every evening to mindful breathing (see exercise 6.6). In addition, he practices mindfulness during his commute on the train.

After two months of mindfulness practice, he begins to notice a pattern to his thoughts and feelings that involves his perfectionism, his tendency to ruminate, and how his rumination affects his mood and performance: When his work performance isn't perfect, he tends to ruminate about it and then feel sad. Over time, this leads him to feel more depressed, and he is not as effective at work. For example, a month ago he gave a lecture that didn't go as well as expected. Afterward, his boss praised him for aspects of the presentation that went well and also provided several pieces of constructive criticism. However, for the next couple of weeks, Joaquin continually thought about the aspects of his lecture that were not perfect and how he had let down his boss. He lost confidence and became less productive. Consequently, he felt depressed and hopeless about his ability to be a competent teacher.

Through mindfulness practice, Joaquin is able to change this pattern of negative thinking. Instead of ruminating about his mistakes, Joaquin uses mindfulness to focus on the present moment. In doing so, he recognizes the things at work he is doing well, like mentoring students interested in writing careers. This shift of focus creates more positive emotions, increases his self-confidence, and may prevent the onset of another depressive episode.

You can apply mindfulness to almost any type of situation. However, before applying it to everyday experiences, most people find it helpful to master some basic mindfulness exercises. Exercises 6.5 and 6.6 will help you practice the skill of mindfulness so that you can better apply the concept to your daily experiences.

Exercise 6.6.   Mindful Breathing

There are several ways that you can practice mindful breathing. For example, you could designate a specific time each day to breathe and then practice being aware of the moment-to-moment experience. In doing so, you strengthen your ability to focus your attention on something—in this case, your breath—over a period of time. You also learn to be less reactive to the thoughts that pass through your mind. You may want to start off dedicating just one or two minutes to mindful breathing and gradually work your way up to longer. A second way to practice mindful breathing is to do it periodically, such as when you are driving, eating lunch, or riding on the train. Practicing mindful breathing when you are not very stressed will put you in a better position to use it during times of stress, when you are most prone to engage in rumination or unhealthy coping behaviors. Here are some instructions to help you practice mindful breathing.

1. Bring your attention to your body and mind. Pay attention to what you are thinking and feeling, both physically and emotionally. Observe these sensations without judging.

2. Bring your attention to your breath. Focus on the physical sensations of the air coming in through your nose, traveling down through your windpipe and lungs and into your diaphragm. Now notice the sensation of the air coming back out from your diaphragm and lungs and out through your nostrils.

3. Inevitably, your attention will wander away from your breathing; when it does, do not judge yourself for it, but gently bring your attention back to your breath.

4. Continue to focus on your breath and the process of breathing for several minutes.

Exercise and Nutrition

If you are like many Americans, you may find it difficult to eat well and exercise on a regular basis. So, you may be wondering, *Is it really worth it to try to incorporate changes in my lifestyle while also learning the other mood management skills in this book?* The answer is yes! First, given that you have BPII, you may be at increased risk for physical health problems (Kilbourne et al. 2007); second, exercise and eating well may improve your mood; third, exercise in particular can be very helpful in practicing mindfulness of bodily sensations, because exercise often enhances your physical sensations (causing heavy breathing, sweating, rapid heart rate, etc.). Thus, some people say that they are very focused on the present moment when they are exercising!

It is not entirely clear why individuals with bipolar disorder may be at increased risk for physical health issues, such as heart disease, but there are likely several factors. These factors include side effects of the medications used to treat bipolar disorder; a possible biological or genetic vulnerability to health problems; and higher rates of sedentary lifestyle and poor nutrition, thought to be due to the increased difficulty of exercising and eating well when depressed (Kilbourne et al. 2007; Elmslie et al. 2001; Soreca, Frank, and Kupfer 2009).

You are probably aware of the physical health benefits of exercise and eating well, but you may not be aware of the important benefits that exercise and nutrition can have for your *mental* health. Reviews of research studies have found that exercise can significantly improve depression (Lawlor and Hopker 2001; Stathopoulou et al. 2006). A few small studies have found that exercise and a well-balanced diet improve mood specifically in individuals with bipolar disorder (Ng, Dodd, and Berk 2007; Sylvia et al. 2011). Therefore, it is particularly important for you to focus on exercising and eating well, not only because you may be at increased risk for physical health issues, but also because exercise and eating well can help your mood!

We will refer to making changes to your diet and getting regular exercise as ways to create a healthy lifestyle. In addition, we will discuss how changing one area of your lifestyle (e.g., diet) can help with another (e.g., exercise).

How to Make a Healthy Lifestyle

There are five important principles that may help you make changes to your current exercise regimen and diet.

First, begin by making small changes that are sustainable (i.e., changes that you can live with). For example, if you are currently eating a dessert after every meal, then you may decide that you will choose to eat dessert only three times a week. If you have trouble actually making this change (e.g., you continue to eat dessert every night or more than three times a week), then this change is not small enough, so try setting a new goal. Perhaps you could instead make your desserts smaller. It is very important to aim for reasonable goals that you can maintain, because people tend to feel guilty if they do not meet their goals. Meeting your goals, on the other hand, makes you feel good, which should help you continue to set more goals. Remember: no goal or change is too small!

Second, make one change at a time. It can be difficult to make several changes, especially long-term ones, at the same time. For example, deciding to eat fewer desserts, eat fruits twice a day, and exercise five days a week is a lot of changes all at once! Instead, try to make one change each week. Again, if it is too difficult to follow through with these changes once a week, then spread them out even more (e.g., make one change every two weeks), or revise the goal to make it smaller (e.g., eat fruits once a day and exercise twice a week). Remember to set reasonable goals that you are highly likely to accomplish; it is not helpful to set unrealistic goals that you are not likely to meet.

Third, there are no "forbidden foods." This means you should allow yourself to eat any food that you want when dieting. The key is to watch your portion sizes, or the amount that you eat, as opposed to cutting out certain foods entirely from your diet. This principle is based on evidence that it is hard to cut out your favorite foods forever, and, as the first principle says, you should only make changes that are sustainable. If you continue to make changes that you can live with, this will ensure that you will not start eating poorly or reduce your exercise again. For a good guide to learning about portion sizes, see the US Department of Agriculture (USDA) website (www.choose myplate.gov). There are also several references at the end of this book under "Further Reading" that contain helpful tools for portion guidelines and making changes to your diet and exercise more generally.

Fourth, a chain analysis can help you identify the triggers of your unhealthy habits, or your "chain" (in which each "link" leads to your unhealthy habit), as well as identify potential coping skills.

Exercise 6.7. Chain Analysis

Consider an unhealthy habit, or a behavior that you would like to change to improve your lifestyle. It could be not exercising enough, eating poorly, smoking cigarettes, or drinking too much caffeine. What are your triggers? Consider all the thoughts, feelings, and behaviors that may lead to this problem behavior. Next, consider what alternative thoughts or behaviors might serve as coping skills to help you "break your chain," or lead you away from your problem behavior so that you engage in healthier behaviors. It may be helpful to have a friend or doctor help you brainstorm coping skills. Take a look at the following example and then try to do your own chain analysis for one or two problem behaviors.

EXAMPLE OF A CHAIN ANALYSIS

Problem Behavior: Eating dessert every night after dinner	
Triggers	**Coping Skills**
I don't feel full after dinner.	*Remind myself that I don't need more food.*
I eat dinner early, leaving more time to want dessert.	*Eat dinner later or reduce the dessert-type foods in my house to reduce temptation.*
My friend is also eating dessert.	
I want something sweet.	*Refuse dessert in advance (before dinner) to reduce peer pressure.*
I think, I deserve dessert tonight.	*Have nonfat frozen yogurt instead of ice cream.*
I think, I don't care about my weight.	*Consider rewarding myself with something else.*
	Remind myself that my physical and mental health could improve if I skip or eat a healthy dessert.

Goal: *Eat dessert only five nights a week.*

YOUR CHAIN ANALYSIS #1

Problem Behavior:	
Triggers	Coping Skills

Goal:

YOUR CHAIN ANALYSIS #2

Problem Behavior:	
Triggers	Coping Skills

Goal:

The last important principle to making lifestyle changes is to get support! Many people have trouble maintaining positive diet and exercise changes. Therefore, it can be very helpful to seek out others who are trying to make healthy lifestyle changes. If you do not know anyone, your doctor should be able to help you find resources (e.g., support groups) in your area. Similarly, if you are around people who are not supportive of your efforts to make a healthier lifestyle, consider alternative coping strategies, such as cooking and/or eating your meals separately.

Using the Skills in This Book to Make a Healthy Lifestyle

If you have tried the principles we just discussed and you are still having trouble making a healthy lifestyle, consider using the other skills covered in this book to help you. For example, in chapter 3, we discussed the concept of acceptance. Can you see how it may be difficult to accept being overweight, being out of shape, or having a poor diet? Remember that accepting something does not necessarily mean being okay or happy with it. However, acceptance of a poor diet, for example, means that you are acknowledging the poor diet, and this prepares you to make changes toward a healthier lifestyle. Acceptance could be very important to starting your path to a healthier lifestyle. In chapter 5, we discussed skills to help you change your thoughts. If you tend to have many negative and dysfunctional thoughts about your ability to make changes when trying to exercise more and eat well, you may want to refer to that chapter as well.

Chapter Summary:

- When people with BPII feel overwhelmed, they sometimes engage in unhealthy coping strategies, such as doing drugs or overeating.

- Distress tolerance skills are designed to distract you from unpleasant or painful thoughts or memories and keep you from engaging in unhealthy coping strategies.

- Mindfulness is about bringing your awareness to the present moment in a purposeful and nonjudgmental way. It can reduce rumination and therefore help you avoid or curtail depressed moods.

- Exercise and a balanced diet help your physical and mental health.

- The five keys to making a healthy lifestyle are (1) make small changes that you can live with, (2) make one change at a time, (3) there are no "forbidden foods," (4) use chain analyses to identify what leads you to problem behaviors, and (5) find support.

- Many of the mood-management skills taught in this book can also help you make healthy lifestyle changes.

PART 3

How to Manage Hypomanic Episodes

As discussed in chapter 1, hypomania is a defining characteristic of bipolar II disorder (BPII). In order to receive a diagnosis of BPII, you must have experienced at least one episode of hypomania, as well as one episode of depression. In this section of the workbook, we help you recognize the symptoms and triggers of hypomania. We also discuss tools for monitoring your hypomanic symptoms and provide specific suggestions for coping with hypomania.

CHAPTER 7

Hypomania—What Is It?

Very few books discuss or cover strategies for managing hypomania. This is problematic for people with bipolar II disorder (BPII), because hypomania is the hallmark of the disorder. Although people with bipolar I disorder can experience hypomania as well as mania, people with BPII, by definition, only experience hypomania. In this chapter, you will learn more about the symptoms and early warning signs of hypomania, how it differs from mania, how hypomania can seem appealing at times, and why you might want to avoid hypomanic episodes.

Symptoms of Hypomania

As discussed in chapter 1, the symptoms of hypomania are as follows (APA 2013):

- A distinct period of abnormally and persistently elevated, expansive, or irritable mood

- Grand/extravagant style, high self-esteem, or grandiose thoughts

- A decreased need for sleep, or feeling rested with less sleep than usual

- Pressured speech, or feeling more talkative than usual

- Racing thoughts or more ideas than usual

- Distractibility

- An increase in goal-directed activity or excessive restlessness

- Overindulgence in enjoyable behaviors with high risk of a negative outcome

Hypomania is defined as experiencing the first symptom—a distinct period of abnormally and persistently elevated, expansive, or irritable mood—in addition to three of the other symptoms (or four, if the mood is just irritable), for at least four days. Let us now go into more detail about each of these symptoms. We will then explain how these symptoms differ from those of mania.

Abnormally and Persistently Elevated, Expansive, or Irritable Mood

Hypomania can feel similar to being in a very good mood, and is sometimes described as euphoria or the feeling of being on a drug high without actually taking any drugs. When you are hypomanic, people who know you well might notice that you are acting differently than usual. Hypomania can also manifest as a kind of high-energy irritability that may draw you into arguments with friends, family, or even strangers. (This is different from a depressed or "low energy" irritability, in which you may just want to avoid people, as opposed to confronting them.)

Inflated Self-Esteem or Grandiose Thoughts

Inflated self-esteem when you are hypomanic is more than just a healthy sense of self-worth. It often takes the form of believing that you are smarter, more creative, or more physically attractive than others, even though there is no concrete evidence to support such beliefs. For example, you may overestimate the likelihood that the attractive person across the room is interested in you, or you may think you can take on more responsibilities at work than you really have time in your day for. It is important to note that the grandiosity that may accompany a hypomanic episode does not include *delusions*. Delusions refer to irrational beliefs. For example, it is considered delusional to believe that you have the ability to singularly bring about world peace or that you are God. When experiencing hypomania you may have an exaggerated sense of self-esteem, but your beliefs are still rational. For example, you may believe that you can be promoted more quickly than others at work or that you are more intelligent than your friends.

Decreased Need for Sleep

This symptom of hypomania means that you actually *need* less sleep such that you feel rested even though you are sleeping less than usual. For example, if you typically sleep for seven to eight hours per night, when you are experiencing hypomania you may sleep for only four to five hours per night yet not feel tired during the day. You may also find that you have trouble getting to sleep at night or wake up earlier than usual and have trouble getting back to sleep.

Pressured Speech, or Feeling More Talkative Than Usual

This is one of the symptoms of hypomania that other people often notice. When you are hypomanic, you may find that you have more to say than usual and that you are actually talking faster than usual. You may also find that you feel the need to keep talking and that it is actually difficult for you to stop talking; this is what we mean by "pressured speech." People may ask you to slow down because they are having trouble understanding what you are saying or because they are unable to get a word in edgewise. You may also find yourself interrupting others and feeling as though others are talking more slowly.

Racing Thoughts or More Ideas

When you are hypomanic, you may feel as though you have more ideas or thoughts running through your mind than usual. Given that hypomania is often associated with inflated self-esteem, your thoughts may feel more creative, unique, or insightful than usual, and you may want to express each thought verbally because they all seem very important (leading to pressured speech, another hypomanic symptom).

Distractibility

If you tend to be distracted easily under normal conditions, when you are hypomanic this tendency will feel stronger than usual, and you will notice that it is hard to concentrate for too long on any one task, such as reading, watching TV, or writing. You will find yourself very easily distracted by things going on around you, such as the activities of other people, sounds, and lights. This may manifest in starting one activity only to leave it and start another activity before you've finished.

An Increase in Goal-Directed Activity or Excessive Restlessness

This symptom often goes hand-in-hand with the new, creative ideas and energy that you may have when hypomanic. You may find that you are busier, more productive, and more active than usual, and others may take notice. For example, you decide to clean out and rearrange that closet that you've been meaning to tackle for months; or you find yourself socializing with friends every night of the week, when you are typically social only on the weekends.

This symptom can also manifest as restlessness, or *psychomotor agitation*, also known as nervous energy. You may have difficulties sitting still or feel very uncomfortable if you have to make yourself sit still for an extended period of time. Your restlessness may initially take the form of fidgeting with your hands or tapping your foot, but you may progress to pacing in an attempt to diminish the nervous energy.

Overindulgence in Enjoyable Behaviors with High Risk of a Negative Outcome

This is another hypomanic symptom that often catches other people's attention. If you are experiencing this symptom, you will have the urge to engage in behaviors that are unusual for you and possibly risky. For example, you are normally a cautious driver, but you find yourself enjoying the thrill of speeding on the highway. You may spend more money on clothes and accessories than is typical for you or find yourself drinking more alcohol than usual.

Hypomania vs. Mania

As shown in table 1.1, the symptoms of a hypomanic episode are the same as those of a manic episode. However, in mania these symptoms are more extreme—they last longer and lead to significant impairment at work, at home, or in relationships or result in hospitalization (APA 2013) (for a review of these symptoms, see chapter 1). For example, in mania, the symptom of decreased need for sleep may manifest as not sleeping at all for several days, or the symptom of grandiosity may manifest as delusions (irrational beliefs). In addition, the symptoms last at least seven days, as opposed to four.

To illustrate how these symptoms can come together in a hypomanic episode, we present Cassandra's story. Think about her signs and symptoms and see whether you can relate to any of them.

• Cassandra

Cassandra, a thirty-eight-year-old paralegal, was diagnosed with BPII ten years ago. Although she is single, she is close with her family and has always had lots of friends. Before she was diagnosed with BPII, she thought of herself as continually on an emotional roller coaster. She would go through periods of depression, in which she would lose interest in her hobbies (rowing and guitar), experience terrible insomnia, and have thoughts that life was not worth living. During these times, she would withdraw from family and friends, frequently call in sick to work, and go into what she called her "shell." But she also had periods of mood elevation, which she called her "highs." When she felt this way, she felt terrific! These periods usually started with her feeling more energetic and sleeping less. She found herself waking up at 4:00 a.m., rather than her usual 7:00 a.m. A few days after experiencing the decreased need for sleep, she would start to take on more activities and responsibilities; during one of her "highs" she organized a food drive at her work and decided to run for treasurer of her local Junior League chapter. During another one of her "highs" she decided to start training for a marathon, even though she had never run more than three miles. Another time, she volunteered to reorganize the closets of several of her girlfriends. Her friends would joke with her that she was a "machine" because she started so many tasks, although Cassandra found that she had difficulty finishing many of them. She frequently became frustrated that people around her seemed slower than her, and she had difficulty focusing on what they were saying because she became easily distracted. She felt as though she had several new, good ideas, but when she shared them with others, her friends and coworkers would complain that she was being too talkative.

Early Warning Signs

For most people with BPII, hypomania doesn't arrive out of the blue; rather, the symptoms gradually build up over the course of several days or even weeks. In our clinical experience, most people who carefully follow their mood episodes learn to identify a few specific symptoms that show up first, known as *early warning signs*. For Cassandra, her early warning signs were increased energy and decreased need for sleep. We discussed early warning signs of depression in chapter 5, and the logic is the same with hypomania; early warning signs are the first visible symptoms of hypomania. Thus, the earlier that you can "catch" the symptoms of hypomania, the better chance you have of preventing a full-blown hypomanic episode.

Not every person who experiences hypomania will experience the same set of symptoms. The first step toward better management of your hypomania is to identify your particular signs and symptoms, as well as your early warning signs.

Exercise 7.1.   Your Specific Symptoms of Hypomania

Use the following table to identify which symptoms characterize your hypomanic episodes. Place a check mark in the "Early Warning Sign" column if this symptom is one of the first to appear for you. In the "Personal Example" column, briefly describe how this symptom affects you. For example, if the symptom is an increase in goal-directed activity, your personal example may be the time you stayed up all night cleaning and rearranging your best friend's garage.

Symptom	Have I Experienced This Symptom? (√)	Early Warning Sign? (√)	Personal Example	Did It Cause Significant Impairment or Problems for Me? (√)
A distinct period of abnormally and persistently elevated, expansive, or irritable mood, lasting at least four days				
Inflated self-esteem or grandiose thoughts				
A decreased need for sleep				
Pressured speech, or feeling more talkative than usual				
Racing thoughts, or more ideas				
Distractibility				
An increase in goal-directed activity or excessive restlessness				
Overindulgence in enjoyable behaviors with high risk of a negative outcome				

As a reminder, for these symptoms to qualify as a hypomanic *episode*, you must have endorsed the first symptom listed plus three additional symptoms (four additional symptoms if your mood is irritable instead of elevated). These symptoms must also have occurred at the same time and lasted at least four days, and none of these symptoms should have caused significant impairment or problems for you (APA 2013). (For a full review of the criteria for a hypomanic episode, see chapter 1.)

How Your Thinking Changes When You Are Hypomanic

In chapter 5, we discussed the impact that depression can have on your thinking. Similarly, mood elevation, or hypomania, can also have a profound effect on your thoughts. Hypomania can put "rose-colored glasses" on you; in other words, it can cause you to have an overly optimistic view of yourself, your world, and your future. Your opportunities may appear endless, and you may feel as if anything is possible. You might feel more attractive or more trusting of strangers. You may become more impulsive and take risks or spend more money than you should. These types of thoughts are called *hyperpositive thoughts*. While it may feel wonderful to think this way, these types of thoughts can cause difficulty for you. For example, it may be tough for your close friends and family to cope with the unpredictability of your thinking or you may do something that you will regret.

Irritable thoughts can also be a component of hypomania. When you are hypomanic, you may tend to interpret situations in a way that could cause you to feel easily angered or annoyed. You may get more frustrated about waiting in lines or dealing with traffic. You may also have less patience with loved ones and be more likely to snap at them.

The tools that we discuss in this chapter will assist you in evaluating your hyperpositive thoughts. Chapter 8 will go into detail about specific strategies for managing your hyperpositive thoughts.

As we have discussed in previous chapters, thoughts, feelings, and behaviors are highly interconnected. The way that you think about yourself or a situation influences your mood and behavior.

In exercise 7.2 are examples of typical hyperpositive thoughts and potential behaviors associated with hypomania. While optimistic thinking can certainly be helpful in many situations, we'd like to caution you regarding the potential downsides to *"unhealthy" optimism*. For example, if you prepared well and worked very hard on a big project at work, it might be perfectly reasonable (and helpful) to feel confident or optimistic about the outcome. However, in hypomania, there is sometimes the tendency to be overly confident or positive, without the preparation or evidence to back up your thinking. This "unhealthy" optimism may lead to potentially negative behaviors or negative outcomes (see exercise 7.2).

Exercise 7.2.   Checklist: Your Hyperpositive Thoughts and Associated Behaviors

Identify which of the following thoughts you have when you are hypomanic. In the blank spaces at the bottom of the list, fill in other typical thoughts you have when you are feeling hypomanic and potentially negative behaviors that go along with those thoughts.

_____ *Everything is going to work out perfectly.*

- Risk taking
- Lack of attention to details

_____ *Everyone is attracted to me.*

- Inappropriate flirting
- Wearing seductive clothing in inappropriate situations
- Embarrassment
- Trouble in relationships

_____ *I should always live for the moment.*

- Risk taking
- Overspending
- Ignoring important responsibilities
- Trusting strangers

_____ *I want it now.*

- Impatience
- Impulsivity
- Irritability

_____ *I am smarter than everyone else.*

- Arrogance
- Lack of respect for others

_____ *My idea is guaranteed to lead to success.*

- Risk taking
- Impulsivity

_____ *Everyone else is moving so slowly and taking so long.*

- Impatience

- Irritability

- Anger

_____ *Other people do not know how to have fun.*

- Risk taking

- Alienating others

- Irritability

_____ *I have so many important things to say.*

- Talking rapidly

- Interrupting others

_____ *I do not need to sleep. I have too many things to do.*

- Lack of sleep

- Further mood instability

- Negative impact on physical health

_____ *I am hilarious.*

- Inappropriate humor

- Embarrassment

_____ *My medications are not important.*

- Further mood instability

_____   _____

- _____

- _____

_____   _____

- _____

- _____

Why You Might Want to Avoid Hypomanic Episodes

As you have learned, the main difference between mania and hypomania is the severity and duration of symptoms and the degree to which they impact your life. In other words, hypomanic episodes are not as severe or long lasting as manic episodes, and they do not seriously affect your ability to manage your life. As a result, some people believe that hypomania is an enjoyable and desirable state. So, why would anyone want to avoid the good feelings and productivity that can come with hypomania? This is a very important question. Despite the potential attractiveness of hypomania, there are good reasons to consider minimizing its occurrence.

Negative Consequences

Hypomania does not lead to significant difficulty in your ability to do things; however, that is not to say that it can't cause some problems or at the very least, some embarrassing moments. Hypomania can lead to impulsivity, poor decision making, and inappropriate behavior, all of which may negatively affect your relationships. For example, you may become hypersexual and, despite being married, make sexual advances toward a friend. This could upset your partner and be very embarrassing for you and your friend. A prominent businessman we know became very talkative during an episode of hypomania and had difficulties "turning himself off" in meetings and on phone calls. During an important meeting with a client, he inappropriately dominated the conversation to the point that the client became irritated. As a result, his boss had a talk with him about the need to monitor himself more carefully. While these situations might not result in serious negative consequences, you can see how they might best be avoided.

Hypomania can also be dangerous because it is associated with your disorder, which means that it is also associated with depression. The relationship between depression and hypomania is not entirely clear, but people often describe "crashing" into a depression immediately after a hypomanic episode. For this reason, hypomania can signal a worsening course of illness, and evidence suggests that the more mood episodes you have, the more difficult the disorder is to treat over time (Scott et al. 2006). It's as if each episode wears down the body or stresses it more, making it more difficult to manage the illness. In short, because hypomania can destabilize many aspects of your life, it is best to minimize its occurrence.

Hypomania → Mania

If you've been diagnosed with BPII, you have never experienced a manic episode; however, there is a possibility that you *could* experience mania. For example, one recent study followed individuals diagnosed with BPII over a period of several years and found that approximately 17 percent (or almost 1 in 5) went on to have a manic episode (Alloy et al. 2012). This does not necessarily mean that your BPII will turn into BPI, but it does highlight the importance of being vigilant in monitoring and understanding your hypomania. It may be helpful for you to think about some of the behaviors you have displayed when hypomanic, the consequences of those behaviors, and how motivated you are to avoid future occurrences.

Monitoring Your Symptoms of Hypomania

Before you learn specific strategies that can help with hypomania in chapter 8, we recommend that you begin using the Daily Diary Card, which we introduced in chapter 4 in the context of depression.

As we discussed in chapter 4, one of the best ways to develop an understanding of your symptoms is to track your mood on a daily basis. Use of the Daily Diary Card can help you better understand your particular signs and symptoms of hypomania and how daily stressors, sleep changes, and medications are all related to your mood. In addition, regular use of the Daily Diary Card will help you keep track of and monitor the effects of your medication use.

Please note that the range of possible responses in the "Mood Tracking" section of the Daily Diary Card goes all the way to "Severely Elevated (Significant Impairment/Unable to Work)." By definition, mood elevation in people with BPII does not cause impairment or inability to work. However, we have left this rating of "Severely Elevated" on the form in the event that you do experience more severe mood elevation symptoms that lead to impairment. If you do experience significant interference from mood elevation, you are likely experiencing mania, rather than hypomania, and may have BPI rather than BPII.

Also, please note we don't expect you to be able to fill in the last section of the Daily Diary Card, "Skills I Used Today to Manage My Mood," because we have not yet discussed strategies for managing hypomania. So you can leave this section blank until you have read chapter 8, in which such strategies are discussed.

DAILY DIARY CARD

Date: _____

FEMALES ONLY: Did you have menstrual flow today? _____

- What was the first day of your last period? _____

Last night's SLEEP

- Time you went to bed last night: _____

- Time you woke up this morning: _____

Any naps today? _____

_____

Did you sleep through the night? _____

_____

Did you have energy that sustained you throughout the day? _____

_____

ADDITIONAL NOTES ON SLEEP

_____

_____

MEDICATIONS TAKEN TODAY

1. _____

2. _____

3. _____

4. _____

5. _____

6. _____

7. _____

8. _____

ADDITIONAL NOTES ON MEDICATIONS

MOOD TRACKING (Check one)

_____ +3 SEVERELY ELEVATED (Significant Impairment; Not Able to Work)

_____ +2 MODERATELY ELEVATED (Significant Impairment; Able to Work)

_____ +1 MILDLY ELEVATED (No Significant Impairment; Able to Work)

_____ ±0 BASELINE ("Normal"/Grounded/Capable & Able/Productive)

_____ –1 MILDLY DEPRESSED (No Significant Impairment)

_____ –2 MODERATELY DEPRESSED (Significant Impairment; Able to Work)

_____ –3 SEVERELY DEPRESSED (Significant Impairment; Not Able to Work)

Any thoughts of suicide today? _____

Anxiety Rating*: _____	COMMENTS:
Irritability Rating*: _____	COMMENTS:

* Rating ➔ 0 = NONE, 1 = MILD, 2 = MODERATE, 3 = SEVERE

ADDITIONAL NOTES ON MOOD

Description of My Day

_____

_____

_____

Skills I Used Today to Manage My Mood

_____

_____

_____

Chapter Summary:

- Hypomania consists of a distinct period of abnormally and persistently elevated or irritable mood (in addition to other symptoms) lasting at least four days.

- To prevent hypomanic episodes, it is important to identify your specific early warning signs.

- In hypomania, thoughts can become positively biased; these types of thoughts are known as hyperpositive thoughts.

- Hypomania may feel enjoyable or pleasurable at times.

- Hypomania can lead to impulsivity, poor decision making, interpersonal difficulties, and, in some cases, depression and mania.

CHAPTER 8

Taking Action to Manage Your Hypomania

In chapter 7, we discussed ways to recognize and understand your hypomania. Now, we will focus on strategies that you can use to challenge your thoughts, stabilize your mood, and gain control over your behaviors.

Modifying Hyperpositive Thinking

Chapter 7 discussed how the specific symptoms of hypomania can affect your thinking. Specifically, you learned that hypomania can have a significant effect on your thoughts such that you view things in an unrealistically positive way and experience *hyperpositive thoughts*. Indeed, hypomania can make you look at yourself, your world, and your future through rose-colored glasses.

If you recall from chapter 5, you can use Automatic Thought Records to track and modify your negative thinking. Automatic Thought Records can also be extremely useful in tracking and modifying hyperpositive thinking. As discussed in chapter 5, the best way to notice your thinking patterns is to identify what we call *automatic thoughts*. Automatic thoughts are thoughts that seem to arise on their own in response to events or situations. These automatic thoughts occur so naturally and frequently that they can actually be difficult to track. This can be especially true when you are hypomanic, because during such times you have more automatic thoughts and they come very quickly. Thus, often the best way to tune in to your automatic thoughts when you are hypomanic is to pay close attention to your mood. When you have a change in mood, ask yourself, *What thought just went through my mind?*

The goal of tracking your hyperpositive automatic thoughts is to help you distinguish between healthy and unhealthy optimism. Healthy optimistic thoughts have evidence to support them and tend to have fewer potentially negative associated behaviors. Unhealthy optimistic thoughts do not have much evidence to support them, often have potentially negative associated behaviors—or negative consequences—and may be overly grandiose, or too optimistic. As discussed in chapter 5, challenging your thoughts and changing unrealistic thoughts is referred to as *cognitive restructuring*.

You may wish to review chapter 5 to brush up on your cognitive restructuring skills. However, what follows here is an example of how to use cognitive restructuring to gain a more balanced perspective on hyperpositive thoughts. For hypomania, the cognitive errors are in the positive direction, rather than the negative. For example, to jump to conclusions would be to jump to a positive conclusion, and "Discounting the Positives" would be instead "Discounting the Negatives."

Example Hyperpositive Automatic Thought Record

Part 1

Situation (Who/What/Where/When)

Presenting at a work meeting

Automatic Thought

What was going through my mind just before I began to feel hyperpositive? What does that mean about me? What does this mean about me in the big picture (my life and future)? What does this suggest in terms of what the other person might think or feel about me? Or, what does this mean about the other person or people in general?

My ideas are better than anyone else's.

How much do I believe this automatic thought? (0–100%) *100%*

Cognitive Errors (Circle all that apply.)

Fortune Telling	Mind Reading	Catastrophizing
All-or-Nothing Thinking	Mental Filter	Personalizing
(Jumping to Conclusions)	Overgeneralizing	(Magnifying or Minimizing)
(Discounting the Positives)	Labeling	Should-Statements
Emotional Reasoning		

Emotion	Strength (1–100)
Elation	*80*
Frustration	*80*
(at having to listen to others)	

Part 2

What is the objective evidence that my thought is true?

There is really no evidence that my ideas are the only good ideas. (90%)

What are some alternatives that might help explain the situation?

I have bright colleagues who contribute to my ideas. (80%)

If a friend were in this situation and had this thought, what would I tell him or her?

Even though you are proud of your ideas, you work as part of a team and you need to listen to others. (90%)

What is the effect of this thought on my mood? Are there any benefits? Are there any costs?

My ideas will be better received if I do not act arrogantly. (90%)

What's the worst that could happen if this thought is true? What's the best that could happen? What's the most realistic outcome?

While this thought might make me feel more confident, the downside is that I might come across as arrogant or disrespectful of others. (100%)

How much do I believe this automatic thought now? (0–100%) 50%

Emotion	**Strength** (1–100)
Elation	*50*
Frustration	*10*

Balanced or Healthier Thought

Even though I have great ideas, I will benefit from listening to my colleagues and incorporating feedback. My ideas will be better received if I do not diminish the contributions of others. (90%)

Your goal in using the Hyperpositive Automatic Thought Record is to systematically question and test out your hyperpositive automatic thought and to construct a more balanced response to the event or situation. The preceding example illustrates how you can train yourself to track your hyperpositive thinking, modify your thoughts to increase their accuracy, and, consequently, reduce potentially negative behaviors. Distinguishing between healthy and unhealthy optimism can help you maximize your self-confidence and success, without alienating others or taking unnecessary risks.

Exercise 8.1. Hyperpositive Automatic Thought Record

Now, it's your turn to use one of your examples and practice responding to your hyperpositive automatic thoughts using the following worksheet. Remember, that the cognitive errors for hypomania are in the positive direction. An electronic version is available at http://www .newharbinger.com/27664 (see the back of this book for more information).

Part 1

Situation (Who/What/Where/When)

_____

_____

Automatic Thought

What was going through my mind just before I began to feel hyperpositive? What does that mean about me? What does this mean about me in the big picture (my life and future)? What does this suggest in terms of what the other person might think or feel about me? Or, what does this mean about the other person or people in general?

_____

How much do I believe this automatic thought? (0–100%) _____

Cognitive Errors (Circle all that apply.)

Fortune Telling	Mind Reading	Catastrophizing
All-or-Nothing Thinking	Mental Filter	Personalizing
Jumping to Conclusions	Overgeneralizing	Magnifying or Minimizing
Discounting the Positives	Labeling	Should-Statements
Emotional Reasoning		

Emotion	Strength (1–100)
_____	_____
_____	_____
_____	_____

Part 2

What is the objective evidence that my thought is true?

_____

_____

What are some alternatives that might help explain the situation?

_____

_____

If a friend were in this situation and had this thought, what would I tell him or her?

_____

_____

What is the effect of this thought on my mood? Are there any benefits? Are there any costs?

_____

_____

What's the worst that could happen if this thought is true? What's the best that could happen? What's the most realistic outcome?

_____

_____

How much do I believe this automatic thought now? (0–100%) _____

Emotion	Strength (1–100)
_____	_____
_____	_____
_____	_____

Balanced or Healthier Thought

_____

_____

Strategies for Managing Hypomanic Behaviors

So far in this chapter, we have discussed ways to modify hyperpositive thinking. Now, we turn our focus to behavioral strategies that can minimize any potential downsides to hypomania.

As mentioned in chapter 7, impulsivity can be a major component of hypomania, and it can lead you to do or say things quickly, without weighing the pros and cons of your behavior. Even though, by definition, hypomanic episodes are not associated with severe impairments, such as hospitalization or job loss, impulsive behaviors associated with hypomania can contribute to problems at work and in relationships. For example, if you speak rapidly or frequently interrupt, it can be frustrating to those around you. Hypomania can sometimes lead you to make impulsive jokes or comments that could be inappropriate. While quick decision making may at times be exciting, the unpredictability it creates can be problematic in some relationships. Impulse purchases (even if they are within your budget and cause no adverse financial impact) may cause you regret.

Exercise 8.2. Identifying Your Impulsive Behaviors

Think about which types of impulsive behaviors you have displayed during previous hypomanic episodes. Ask yourself the following questions, and write your answers in the spaces below.

What impulsive behaviors have I displayed when hypomanic?

_____

_____

_____

_____

Were there any downsides or negative consequences of these behaviors?

_____

_____

_____

_____

Did friends or family members comment on my behaviors? If so, what did they say?

_____

_____

_____

_____

Reducing Impulsivity

The following strategies are designed to reduce impulsive decision making and minimize the regret sometimes associated with hypomanic behavior.

THE TWO-PERSON FEEDBACK RULE

The Two-Person Feedback Rule (Newman et al. 2002) encourages you to check with two trusted friends or family members before making any major life decision. As we have discussed, hypomania can lead to impulsive decision making, so this strategy encourages you to get input from at least two trusted sources before doing something that you might regret. So, before quitting your job, doing something new or very different, or buying something expensive, we recommend that you utilize your support system carefully. Most CEOs and presidents have a "cabinet" of advisors. Are your decisions that affect your life any less important than the ones they make?

THE FORTY-EIGHT HOURS BEFORE ACTING RULE

Along with checking out your life decisions with two trusted sources, we also recommend utilizing the Forty-Eight Hours Before Acting Rule (Newman et al. 2002). This strategy encourages you to wait at least two full days _and_ get two full nights of sleep before acting on your big plans. We know that sleep loss can drive hypomania, so you should "sleep on it" for at least two nights before making a major decision.

The Bipolar II Disorder Workbook

LIMIT YOUR ACCESS TO FUNDS

Some people have increased impulsivity with regard to spending when they are hypomanic. If impulsive spending has been an issue for you in the past (even if it has not caused serious problems), you may wish to consider giving your credit cards to a trusted person when you feel hypomanic. One strategy involves literally putting your credit cards in some water and storing them in the freezer. In the time that it takes to thaw your cards, you will have a chance to reevaluate the necessity of your purchase. Also, consider deleting any credit card information you have stored with online retailers or other shopping sites, so that it is not so easy to make impulsive purchases. Similarly, look into disabling any online payment system accounts or making them harder to use. Most importantly, avoid purchasing nonreturnable items.

AVOID CONFRONTATION

If you are feeling hypomanic, avoid interacting with people who trigger you or typically cause you to feel irritated. Increased irritability is often a symptom of hypomania, and your patience and tolerance for difficult people or situations may be lessened. For example, you may want to avoid interacting with your ex-partner when feeling hypomanic.

THINK BEFORE SPEAKING OR E-MAILING

When you are hypomanic, your thoughts and speech might be accelerated and, as a result, you may be more likely to blurt out something impulsively. If your mood feels high, try waiting at least five seconds before speaking to allow yourself time to carefully think through what you would like to say. You may also feel more humorous when hypomanic, so it is a good idea to censor your jokes or think them through carefully before you share them. The ability to listen attentively also tends to diminish during hypomania, so try to be especially aware of whether you are listening to others. In addition to thinking before speaking, we recommend waiting and thinking very carefully before firing off an angry or impulsive e-mail. The Two-Person Feedback Rule and/or the Forty-Eight Hours Before Acting Rule can also be very helpful in saying and writing the right things!

AVOID ALCOHOL AND DRUGS

It is always wise to minimize your use of alcohol and avoid the use of recreational drugs. This is especially true when you are hypomanic. When you are hypomanic, alcohol and recreational drugs can increase your chances of engaging in risky, impulsive, or dangerous behavior.

We reviewed several behavioral strategies that may help you manage impulsive behavior. Now, think about your life and what may work best for you. Are there certain times when one strategy may be better than another? For example, perhaps while traveling it is harder for you to limit your access to funds, so you may need to be very careful and use other strategies during this time.

Exercise 8.3. Strategies for Reducing Impulsivity

Think about which of the strategies discussed in this section will be most helpful to you and why. Other people can be very helpful when you are trying to learn new skills, so try to identify people who could help you with specific strategies. Ask yourself the following questions, and write your answers in the spaces below.

What strategies do I plan to use to reduce my impulsivity associated with hypomania? Why? When?

_____

_____

_____

_____

_____

_____

Who are some trusted family members or friends that I might be able to enlist to help me? Who would help me with which strategies?

_____

_____

_____

_____

_____

_____

Sleep

In previous chapters, we discussed the importance of maintaining a regular sleep cycle in order to stabilize your mood. This is particularly important with regard to hypomania, because decreased sleep can trigger hypomanic episodes (Wehr, Sack, and Rosenthal 1987). For example, losing sleep due to working late into the night, due to traveling (jet lag), or due to going out with friends can cause your mood to become elevated.

In addition to being a *trigger* for hypomania, a decreased need for sleep is also a *symptom* of hypomania. Therefore, you may feel rested after having only a small amount of sleep. As a result, you may be tempted to stay up later, because you may not feel tired. Furthermore, you may have more energy in the evening (this is quite common in people experiencing hypomania), so winding down your nighttime activities (e.g., turning off the TV/computer and preparing for bed) may be particularly challenging. You may also have thoughts that sleep is not that important. For example, you might think, *Why go to sleep when I can be so productive?* However, sleep loss, over time, can take a serious toll on your mood stability and physical health.

The following strategies can help you protect your sleep when you are hypomanic:

Minimize stimulation. Taking a break, or reducing stimulation, can be very helpful in quieting hypomania and preparing for sleep. For example, decreasing exposure to light, loud noises, computers, and televisions can have a soothing and calming effect. Try to "unplug" from these stimulating activities at least thirty minutes before your desired bedtime. Also, avoid watching TV in bed, and only get into bed when you are ready for sleep.

Do relaxation exercises. Some of the exercises described later in this book (chapter 10), such as diaphragmatic breathing or imagery, can help you relax before bed. These types of exercises will teach you to slow your breathing and relax various muscle groups. You may find that engaging in these relaxation exercises while lying in bed can help you drift off to sleep more peacefully.

Minimize caffeine. Caffeine use, particularly later in the day, can dramatically interfere with your ability to sleep. When you are hypomanic, it is wise to carefully limit your intake of caffeinated beverages, such as coffee, tea, and soda.

Challenge dysfunctional thoughts about sleep. If you are having thoughts that sleep is not that important, or really doesn't matter that much, or may reduce your productivity or fun, consider weighing the pros and cons of such thoughts by using an Automatic Thought Record.

Consult your doctor about medication. If you are having difficulty sleeping, it is always wise to speak with your doctor. Your doctor might prescribe an additional medication to help you sleep.

Managing Medications

Some people, when hypomanic, feel "on top of the world" or "really happy" and begin to question the usefulness of their medications. They may decide that they no longer need to take their medications. As described in chapter 2, medications are an essential part of successfully managing bipolar II disorder (BPII). If you are questioning the importance of your medication, we encourage you to speak with your doctor and/or therapist about your concerns. We also recommend challenging your beliefs about medication by using an Automatic Thought Record.

Distractibility is quite common in hypomania, and, thus, you may be more likely to forget to take your medications when experiencing hypomania. For this reason, it may be particularly important to track your medication use and set regular reminders.

Using These Skills to Manage Hypomania and Prevent Relapse

In this chapter, we have discussed the importance of using tools to manage your hypomania and decrease any potential downsides to mood elevation. Many of these strategies can also be helpful in preventing relapse and keeping your mood stable.

As discussed in chapter 7, for most people with BPII, hypomania doesn't arrive all at once; rather, the symptoms gradually build up over the course of several days or even weeks. In addition, most people learn to identify a few specific symptoms that show up before the others, known as *early warning signs*. We recommend that you take a moment to review exercise 7.1, in which you identified your early warning signs, before proceeding to exercise 8.4.

Exercise 8.4.   Tools for Coping with Hypomania and Preventing Relapse

Generally, early warning signs of hypomania can also be thought of as mild symptoms. There are also moderate and severe symptoms, which tend to build after you experience mild symptoms. Think about what your mild, moderate, and severe symptoms may be. Then, think about how you can use the tools discussed in this chapter to intervene at each stage of hypomania. In addition, think about how these strategies can help you prevent hypomanic episodes. The following questions will help you summarize your plan to manage the various stages of hypomania and prevent relapse.

When I am in the *mild or very early stages of hypomania*, I experience the following symptoms:

_____

_____

_____

_____

Tools I can use to help myself during mild hypomania:

_____

_____

_____

_____

When I feel *moderately hypomanic*, I experience the following symptoms:

_____

_____

_____

Tools I can use to help myself during moderate hypomania:

_____

_____

_____

_____

When I am *severely hypomanic*, I experience the following symptoms:

_____

_____

_____

_____

Tools I can use to help myself during severe hypomania:

_____

_____

_____

_____

Relapse Prevention

Tools I can use every day to stay well and minimize hypomania:

_____

_____

_____

_____

Chapter Summary:

- Hypomania can lead to hyperpositive thinking and unhealthy optimism, which can be associated with problematic or potentially negative behaviors.

- Automatic Thought Records can help you weigh the pros and cons of your thinking and develop more balanced responses to events and situations.

- Recognizing and reducing the impulsivity associated with your hypomania can help you avoid decisions and behaviors that you might regret.

- Adhering to regular sleep patterns and taking medication on schedule may be particularly challenging when you are hypomanic.

- The tools described in this chapter can help you prevent relapse, or avoid hypomanic episodes, as well as better manage hypomania.

PART 4

How to Manage Anxiety

Although it is not a symptom specific to bipolar II disorder (BPII), many people with BPII suffer from anxiety. In this section of the workbook, we help you better understand what anxiety is and whether anxiety is particularly problematic for you. We also discuss tools for coping with anxiety.

CHAPTER 9

Anxiety—What Is It?

Anxiety disorders are the most common mental illnesses in the United States, affecting around 18 percent of the population in any given year and almost 30 percent of adults in their lifetime (Kessler et al. 2005). Therefore, it is perhaps not surprising that nearly half (46%) of people with bipolar II disorder (BPII) experience anxiety at some point in their life. In fact, if you have BPII, you are actually more likely than the average person to have an anxiety disorder (Simon et al. 2004). Therefore, we devote this chapter to defining anxiety and anxiety disorders, and in the next chapter (chapter 10) we will discuss strategies for managing anxiety.

Stress vs. Anxiety vs. Fear

Anxiety is different from stress or fear; however, these experiences are often confused because they can cause the same physical sensations. Yet, the triggers, or what causes anxiety, stress, or fear, are quite different.

Stress comes from the daily hassles of life, such as issues at work, relationship conflict, or anything else that puts pressure on the mind and body. You experience stress when you perceive that the demands of a particular situation exceed your personal and social resources, such that you believe that you will have difficulty managing the situation. In other words, people tend to experience great stress when they feel as if they don't have the time, experience, or resources to manage a situation. Stress is therefore a negative experience, yet one that depends largely on perceptions. That is to say, stress is never an inevitable, or necessary, consequence of any event. For example, buying nice clothes for a new job may cause you stress if you believe that you do not have enough money to pay your bills; yet it may be fun to buy new clothes if you believe that you have plenty of money. Acute stress, or stress experienced in response to a particular stressor, may build up over time to become chronic stress, and chronic stress can lead to anxiety. Therefore, anxiety can be a response to chronic stress.

Anxiety is a future-focused emotion, often experienced when you are imagining a scary or threatening possible situation. In contrast, fear is a present-focused emotion. Fear is what you experience when you are *in the midst of* a scary or threatening situation. For example, if you were hiking in the woods and saw a big bear, you would likely experience some fear. If you returned to the same woods a year later, you might feel anxious, because you would be thinking about the possibility of seeing a bear, based on your previous experience. Anxiety puts you on the alert for a possible dangerous situation, even if there isn't a dangerous situation right in front of you.

As another example, if you do not like flying, anxiety is what you experience as you drive to the airport, go through security, and board a plane—when you are thinking about the future event of flying, but you are not actually flying yet. Fear is what you experience when you are actually flying. Put a little differently, anxiety is about what may happen and fear is about what *is* happening. As a result, anxiety tends to be subtler or less intense than fear, but it can also be more chronic or longer lasting.

One of the reasons that you may not enjoy the experience of anxiety or fear is the way it makes your body feel. The unpleasant physical response to anxiety and fear is known as the *fight-or-flight response.* You can think of the fight-or-flight response as the body's natural alarm system. In the same way that a home security system makes a loud noise to alert you that there may be a problem (a break-in), the fight-or-flight response alerts you that something is wrong. However, unlike an expensive alarm system, it is free of charge! It has been part of our makeup since humans first walked the earth, and it plays a very important function in keeping us alive.

Basically the way the fight-or-flight response works is by sending a warning in the form of physical sensations, or changes in the body, whenever you encounter a potentially dangerous or threatening situation. These changes tend to manifest in the following symptoms:

- Sweat/perspiration

- Heart pounding or beating more rapidly

- Nausea/upset stomach

- Muscle tension

- Shortness of breath

- Dizziness

- Narrowing of field of vision (also called "tunnel vision")

- Goose bumps

- A sense of being detached from the situation or of watching it from above

- Dry mouth

- Sensitive hearing

- Cold feet/hands

These may seem like strange responses to a threatening situation, but in fact these symptoms serve an important function: they prepare you to take action (fight) or to leave the situation to avoid harm (take flight), hence the name "fight-or-flight response." The rate and strength of your heartbeat increases in order to supply more oxygen to the large muscles in your arms and legs so that you can react to threats more effectively. In addition, blood flow to other areas, such as your fingers, toes, and brain, decreases. Thus, the physical symptoms of fear that you experience when these changes occur are actually the side effects of the body preparing itself for action.

The fight-or-flight response is automatic, and it needs to be in order for it to be useful. The parts of the brain that respond to threat react without involving the parts involved in deliberation or more complex thought. As an example, think about the bear situation discussed earlier. If you were hiking in the Rocky Mountains and suddenly came across a big bear, your fight-or-flight response would likely kick in, causing sweat, a pounding heart, and so forth, and you would most likely flee the situation. If this response wasn't so automatic (and you had to think carefully about what to do), you would be wasting precious time and putting your life at risk. Therefore, the physical changes your body goes through when you are afraid have a purpose and actually help keep you alive.

Importantly, the body does not discriminate between what is actually threatening—like a big bear in the woods—and what you only *perceive* as threatening, like a job interview. In short, your body relies on your brain to tell it what it should fear. This can be problematic because as we have discussed in previous chapters, your thoughts or perceptions can be distorted or wrong. As a result, you may believe that a future situation will be threatening or scary, which will cause you anxiety, even if the situation will be harmless. So that is why you may feel many of the symptoms of the fight-or-flight response before an important job interview: because you have evaluated the situation as threatening, and therefore your body reacts to this perception.

Although it may feel unpleasant, anxiety can serve a useful function by alerting you that a situation you are facing requires your attention. To continue the example of the important job interview, imagine that you have been unemployed for months and feel optimistic that this job may be the one for you. The anxiety you feel about the upcoming interview (perhaps manifested in tense muscles, difficulty sleeping, and headaches) makes you research the company thoroughly, practice your interviewing skills with a friend, and think of good questions for the interviewer; in other words, you prepare well for this interview, which improves your chances of getting the job. If you didn't feel anxious, you would likely prepare less, which might decrease your chances of getting the job. As another example, when the deadline to pay a bill is approaching, you may begin to feel anxious. This is because paying your bills is important to keeping your car, your phone service, your heat, and so forth. In this situation, the experience of anxiety alerts you that paying your bills is very important to you and thus requires your time and energy. If you didn't experience anxiety, you might not work hard enough to get the money to pay your bills, or perhaps delay paying them.

Table 9.1 summarizes the differences between fear and anxiety.

Table 9.1. Fear vs. Anxiety

	Fear	Anxiety
Type of Threat	Immediate Example: Seeing a bear in the woods	Future Example: Returning to the same woods but not seeing the bear
Physical Response	Acute sense of panic Examples: Excessive sweating, rapid heartbeat, and sharp increase in breathing rate (it may be difficult to "catch your breath")	Chronic tension and arousal Examples: Mild sweating, increase in heart and breathing rate, some blushing, hypervigilance leading to headaches
Function	Survival Example: Running away from the bear	Preparedness Example: Packing your food carefully in advance of the hike so that you do not attract a bear
Intensity/Duration	Intense but short Example: Experienced when in presence of the bear (2–3 min.)	Less intense, but longer lasting Example: Experienced for the entire hike (several hours)

To help you think about how fear and anxiety affect you, and to help you differentiate between the two, complete the following exercise.

Exercise 9.1.   Experiences of Fear vs. Anxiety

Think about different situations that have made you feel fearful. Write them in the first column of the following table. In the second column, write about situations that have made you feel anxious. We included a few examples to help you get started.

Situations That Make Me Fearful	Situations That Make Me Anxious
Seeing a snake while hiking	*Planning my hike in woods with snakes*
Giving a speech at my company	*Writing the speech the night before*
My mother yelling at me	*Thinking about going out to lunch with my mother*

Avoidance

People who experience excessive anxiety tend to engage in *behavioral avoidance*. That is, they try to cope with their anxiety by avoiding situations that they believe could trigger, or worsen, their anxiety. This can cause them great difficulty. Let's consider a couple of examples.

• James

James is afraid of flying and has successfully avoided doing so for the past ten years. He has worked in New York City for the past five years as a reporter for a national newspaper. He has been working extremely hard to find and write the best stories. One day, his boss invites him into her office to inform him that he has been promoted! James is overjoyed, until he learns that he will need to travel to London once per month as part of his new job. Feeling too fearful about flying, James declines the promotion, telling his boss that he prefers to stay in his current position. Thinking that James lacks motivation and drive, his boss fires him.

• Nancy

Nancy gets very anxious about driving on highways. She is comfortable driving around town, but avoids driving anywhere that requires she go on a highway. She recently retired and is very excited to be the nanny for her grandson (her daughter's son), who currently lives on her street. Then her daughter tells her that she and her husband will be moving to a nearby town and will need her to drive out there every day if she is to care for her grandson. Feeling too anxious over the prospect of driving on the highway, Nancy tells her daughter that she can no longer be their nanny. Her daughter is furious. She reduces visits between Nancy and her grandson, and Nancy feels sad and lonely.

Although James and Nancy believed that avoiding anxiety-provoking situations would make their lives less stressful and more enjoyable, you can see that their avoidance actually came with significant costs. Another reason that avoidance is a bad coping strategy for anxiety is because avoiding something actually reinforces that it *should* be feared, so that it becomes more feared over time. For example, James's fear of flying will only become worse the longer that he avoids flying, and similarly Nancy will never overcome her fear of driving on highways if she refuses to drive on highways. We will say more about this vicious cycle of anxiety and avoidance in the next chapter.

Anxiety Disorders

By now you understand why some amount of anxiety is "normal" and also necessary to your survival; however, too much anxiety can become problematic. If your anxiety is quite distressing to you and it consistently interferes with important aspects of your life, such as work or relationships, then your anxiety may be a problem. For example, if your anxiety prevents you from maintaining friendships or causes you to lose your job, this may mean that your anxiety is abnormally high and is, thus, better defined as an anxiety disorder. The following exercise (adapted from Chapman, Gratz, and Tull 2011) will help you determine the nature of your anxiety.

Exercise 9.2. Self-Test: Is Anxiety a Problem for Me?

	Yes (√)	No (√)
1. Do I deliberately avoid certain objects or situations (for example, spiders, elevators, or trains) for fear that they will bring up uncomfortable feelings of anxiety?		
2. Do I find that my anxiety interferes with my ability to get things accomplished or stay on task?		
3. Do I deliberately avoid social situations (for example, parties, job interviews, or public speaking) for fear that I will be negatively judged and experience uncomfortable feelings of anxiety?		
4. Are there certain things that I avoid doing in front of other people, such as eating or writing, because they bring up strong feelings of anxiety?		
5. Do I experience out-of-the-blue "attacks" of anxiety in which I suddenly feel several different physical symptoms of anxiety that are very uncomfortable?		
6. Do I frequently have a hard time leaving my home because it is the only place where I feel as though I can manage my anxiety?		
7. Do I frequently have intrusive, repetitive, troublesome thoughts, such as fearing that I have done something very bad or that I am going to harm someone, and then try really hard to ignore or suppress such thoughts?		
8. Do I find myself frequently engaging in repetitive behaviors to minimize anxiety, such as checking to make sure the oven is off or frequently washing my hands?		
9. Do I find myself experiencing persistent, uncontrollable worry about day-to-day concerns, such as chores and work?		
10. Do I find myself having intrusive thoughts and memories about a traumatic event that I experienced, find myself avoiding things that remind me of the event, or feel a sense of having to be on guard since the event?		

Review your responses. If you have several checks in the "Yes" column, anxiety may be a problem for you, but this doesn't necessarily mean that you have an anxiety disorder. Alternatively, if all of your responses were "no," this doesn't necessarily mean that anxiety is not a problem for you. This is because anxiety can manifest itself in many other ways. So if you think that anxiety may be a problem for you, then you might want to continue reading to learn more about anxiety.

The *Diagnostic and Statistical Manual of Mental Disorders, Fifth Edition* (APA 2013) lists a number of anxiety-related disorders. We will discuss some of the major ones here: generalized anxiety disorder, social phobia, specific phobia, panic disorder, obsessive-compulsive disorder, and post-traumatic stress disorder.

Generalized Anxiety Disorder

People with *generalized anxiety disorder* (GAD) experience chronic, persistent, and uncontrollable worry about a number of real-life, day-to-day concerns (e.g., going to work, paying bills, taking care of the children). People who have GAD specifically report feeling anxious most days for the past six months and they often report having felt anxious or nervous all their lives. The worry is accompanied by physical symptoms, such as restlessness, irritability, or muscle tension. There is often no clear focus to the worry, and the worry causes significant distress or difficulty functioning in important areas of life (e.g., work, friends or family, finances).

Social Anxiety Disorder (Social Phobia)

People with *social phobia* experience intense anxiety and self-consciousness in social situations. These can be a specific type of social situation, such as public speaking or urinating in public restrooms, or they can be more general. If you have social anxiety disorder, you are overly concerned about being negatively evaluated or judged, and, as a result, often avoid social situations. Your social anxiety or avoidance must cause significant distress or interfere with your normal routine in order to be considered social anxiety disorder. For example, if you are anxious about speaking in public, you would not receive a diagnosis of social anxiety disorder unless this anxiety caused problems for you at work, school, or home.

Specific Phobia

Specific phobia involves an intense fear of a particular object or situation such that it is often carefully avoided. Common phobias are a fear of heights, a fear of elevators, a fear of enclosed spaces, a fear of certain medical procedures, a fear of spiders, and a fear of snakes. Similar to other anxiety disorders, this intense fear makes it difficult for people to function in their daily lives.

Panic Disorder

A *panic attack* is a sudden surge of intense fear or discomfort, accompanied by strong physical sensations. People with *panic disorder* experience recurrent, unexpected panic attacks. They also worry about future panic attacks or experience a major change in their behavior related to the attack for at least one month after having a panic attack. Thus, people with panic disorder may avoid activities that bring on physical sensations similar to the symptoms of a panic attack, such as exercise.

Obsessive-Compulsive Disorder

People with *obsessive-compulsive disorder* (OCD) have frequent, intrusive, and troublesome thoughts and ideas ("obsessions") and typically engage in rituals or repetitive behaviors/mental acts ("compulsions") to make the obsessions go away. These obsessions tend to be unusual or strange thoughts, as opposed to the worries of people with GAD. For example, people with OCD may have persistent thoughts that they are going to sexually abuse or hurt a child or that they have done something very bad in the past. Compulsions are a way to manage these obsessions, because they serve as distractions. Compulsions often take the form of repetitive hand washing, counting to a certain number, repeating words silently, or carefully lining up objects in a certain way. Your obsessions or compulsions must cause distress, be time consuming (take up more than one hour per day), or significantly interfere with your regular routine in order for you to be diagnosed with OCD.

Post-Traumatic Stress Disorder

People may develop *post-traumatic stress disorder* (PTSD) after a life-threatening or terrifying event in which they felt powerless or victimized. For example, being physically or sexually assaulted, living in a war zone, or watching another person be killed or seriously hurt could cause PTSD. The symptoms of PTSD include flashbacks about the event, avoidance of any reminders of the event, intrusive thoughts and memories about the event, feeling more easily startled, a sense of being emotionally numb, feeling detached from others, and chronic feelings of being on edge or keyed up.

Chapter Summary:

- It is estimated that almost half of individuals diagnosed with BPII will develop an anxiety disorder at some point in their life.

- Fear is a present-focused emotion, whereas anxiety is a future-focused emotion.

- Anxiety and fear serve an important purpose. They alert you to possible dangers (fear) and important situations (anxiety).

- Avoidance is the most common way that people try to cope with anxiety, but it is not helpful in the long term.

- Having an anxiety disorder means that your anxiety is causing you problems and/or significant distress.

CHAPTER 10

Taking Action to Manage Your Anxiety

Many people with bipolar II disorder (BPII) also suffer from anxiety. In chapter 9, we defined anxiety and discussed how to recognize whether it is a problem for you. This chapter presents a variety of strategies for managing your anxiety. We suggest that you choose just one or two skills from this chapter to focus on and practice for a given time period, perhaps two weeks, so that you really learn how to apply that particular skill or those particular skills. In our experience, when people try to learn too many skills at one time, they are not able to effectively practice any of them. We understand that you may be eager to manage your anxiety, but if you try to learn too many skills at one time, you may have difficulty and conclude in error that the skills are not beneficial. Thus, we suggest that you read through this chapter to decide which skills you'd like to focus on first. Then, go back and read about those skills again and try practicing them. Once you have adequately practiced a skill, you should have a good sense of whether or not it will be useful for you, and then you can start practicing other skills in this chapter to see whether they will be helpful as well.

Avoiding Avoidance: Exposure

In chapter 9, we discussed the notion of avoidance and explained how avoidance can actually lead to increased anxiety and decreased quality of life. We gave the examples of James and Nancy, who so actively avoided the things that made them anxious (flying and driving on the highway, respectively) that they ended up damaging important relationships and missing out on positive, enjoyable aspects of their lives.

One of the best things that people with anxiety can do to reduce their anxiety is to stop avoiding the trigger (Barlow, Allen, and Choate 2004). This may seem counterintuitive, because if something makes you feel anxious and uncomfortable, why would you want to face it? Indeed, it is very natural to want to avoid the things that make you feel uncomfortable or distressed; however, as we mentioned in the previous chapter, the big problem with avoidance is that it keeps anxiety alive and well.

Remember James in chapter 9, who is afraid of flying? Undeniably, on any given day James feels better when he doesn't go on an airplane. However, over the long term, this avoidance keeps his anxiety active, because if James never goes on an airplane, he never has the opportunity to learn through experience that what he fears the most (i.e., the plane crashing) is very unlikely to happen. If you want to reduce your anxiety, you must expose yourself to the thoughts and situations you fear. When you do, your brain will learn to stop turning on the fight-or-flight response (i.e., those uncomfortable physical anxiety symptoms) every time you encounter those thoughts and situations. After repeated exposures—this is key—your brain will gradually figure out that the anxious response is exaggerated in response to the actual threat and that it is not necessary to be on such high alert.

In addition to maintaining your anxiety, avoidance can ironically increase your anxious thoughts. In a well-known study, David Wegner and his colleagues asked participants to purposely not think about a white bear while speaking their thoughts out loud (Wegner et al. 1987). What Wegner and his colleagues found was that these participants mentioned a white bear about once a minute, which was a higher frequency than reported by the people who were not prompted to avoid thinking about a white bear. Since that study, there have been many more studies on *thought suppression*. The general findings are that the more people try not to think about something, the more they think about it. Although it may seem counterintuitive, these findings suggest that the more you try to avoid or suppress your anxious thoughts, the more likely they are to come up. In short, avoidance of thoughts, as well as situations, can actually make your anxiety worse.

In his 1933 inaugural address, President Franklin Roosevelt stated that "the only thing to fear is fear itself" (Roosevelt 1938). He was highlighting just how powerful fear can be. Nevertheless, if you would like to live a more fulfilling life, it is your job to stop avoiding anxiety-provoking situations and instead expose yourself to these situations. This is not easy work. It feels uncomfortable and unpleasant (which is why you have avoided it!), so it takes a particular commitment and self-discipline.

To help you expose yourself to the things that you avoid, first, identify one key situation or thought that makes you feel anxious. It is imperative to be consistent in your exposure to it, so expose yourself to it gradually—over the course of weeks or months. For example, let's consider Nancy (from chapter 9), who gets very anxious about driving on highways. Recall that when Nancy's daughter moved to another town, Nancy told her daughter she could no longer be her grandson's nanny because it would require driving on the highway. Nancy's daughter became angry, and relations between them were strained. To illustrate how exposure can reduce anxiety, let's say that Nancy decides she must "get over" her fear of driving on the highway. Although it feels uncomfortable at first, she forces herself to drive on the highway on a daily basis. At first she drives on the highway for just five minutes per day. When that begins to feel a bit more comfortable, or at least slightly less anxiety provoking, she increases her exposure to ten minutes, and when that feels more comfortable, she increases her exposure to fifteen minutes, and so forth. In doing so, Nancy is gradually exposing herself to driving on the highway. Although it is certainly not a pleasurable experience, Nancy is driving on the highway in manageable chunks of time so that she never feels completely overwhelmed. After a couple of months, she finds that driving on the highway doesn't evoke the same high levels of anxiety that it once did, and she tells her daughter she can be her grandson's nanny. Of course, Nancy may never *love* driving on highways, but because she manages to do it more comfortably, she repairs her relationship with her daughter and is able to have the special experience of caring for her grandson. There are several self-help books in the "Further Reading" section at the end of this book that may be helpful to you in designing your own exposure work. However, if your anxiety seems particularly severe, or you suspect that your anxiety meets criteria for an anxiety disorder, it is best to contact a mental health practitioner.

Mindfulness

You were first introduced to the concept of mindfulness in chapter 6. (You may want to review that section before continuing.) Mindfulness is the practice of observing your thoughts, feelings, and experiences in a compassionate, nonjudgmental, accepting way. In addition to its mood benefits, a number of studies have shown that mindfulness can significantly reduce anxiety and panic (Kabat-Zinn et al. 1992). As discussed in chapter 6, the skill of mindfulness teaches you a way to reduce rumination, so that you don't get stuck on the topics that make you anxious and tense.

Mindfulness begins with being aware of your present experience. For example, if you were driving, you could practice mindfulness by focusing carefully on your surroundings and your physical sensations. You might notice what types of cars are on the road with you, how close the car in front of you is, how it feels to be sitting in the driver's seat, whether you feel hot or cold, and the scenery. Someone not practicing mindfulness when driving may instead be thinking about a grocery list, a phone call from yesterday, or an upcoming meeting. In today's fast-paced world, most people move through their daily lives not paying close attention to anything in particular. You may have had the experience of driving somewhere only to realize when you arrived at your destination that, if someone asked you, you couldn't actually describe how you got there! You couldn't remember the streets you turned down or what you saw as you were driving. This is what it looks like to not be mindful.

A common way to practice mindfulness is to select an everyday activity, such as washing the dishes or brushing your teeth, and do it mindfully (see exercise 6.5, "Mindfully Observing an Everyday Object," for an example). To do something mindfully means to pay close attention to what is happening in the present moment. In this regard, it is helpful to pay attention to each of your five senses. So if you were choosing to wash the dishes mindfully, you would pay attention to how the warm water feels on your skin, the smell of the soap, what the soapy water and dishes look like, and the different sounds they make. When you are mindful, you are paying attention to the present moment, and, as a result, you are not focusing on anxious thoughts (an earlier phone call, an upcoming meeting, etc.). Notice that you are not *avoiding* anxious thoughts, but rather purposely replacing them with other thoughts; this is a very important distinction. Although the purpose of mindfulness is not to become relaxed, this is a common side effect of the practice.

One of the key components of mindfulness is to be *nonjudgmental*, or to not assess or evaluate your performance as either good or bad. When people first try mindfulness, they often judge themselves as either succeeding or failing at being mindful. For example, in practicing mindful breathing (see exercise 6.6, "Mindful Breathing"), you may find yourself concerned about not breathing correctly, feeling as though it is taking forever, concerned about your mind wandering, or feeling anxious. These are all normal responses, but they can make the activity seem challenging. Try to remind yourself that there is no "wrong'" way to do mindful breathing and that it will become easier with practice.

There are many more types of mindfulness-based exercises. Please see the "Further Reading" section at the end of this book for recommendations.

Abdominal Breathing

Most of us don't think twice about *how* we breathe because breathing is such a fundamental part of our daily life, something we do all day every day. As a result, you may not know that the manner in which you breathe is closely related to the level of tension and anxiety you are experiencing. Therefore, learning to breathe effectively is an important anxiety-management tool.

Every time you breathe, you take in oxygen and release carbon dioxide. The transmission of oxygen to the various parts of your body and the right balance of oxygen and carbon dioxide in your bloodstream is vital for keeping you alive. When you are anxious, you may, without realizing it, engage in rapid, irregular, and shallow breathing, which results in too little oxygen reaching your brain. This type of breathing affects the balance and flow of the gases in your body. Consequently, a series of physiological reactions lead to the uncomfortable physical symptoms of anxiety, such as light-headedness, heart palpitations, shortness of breath, numbness, weakness, dizziness, tingling, or agitation (Davis, Eshelman, and McKay 2008).

This shallow chest breathing that occurs when you are anxious or fearful is sometimes referred to as *hyperventilation*. This type of breathing is not harmful, and, in fact, many people breathe this way without realizing it. Hyperventilation is a part of the fight-or-flight response, and its purpose is to protect your body from danger. The physical changes associated with hyperventilation, although uncomfortable, are meant to prepare your body for action and will not harm you.

In contrast to the rapid, irregular, and shallow breathing linked with stress and anxiety, *abdominal* or *diaphragmatic breathing* is a slower, deeper, and more regular pattern. To imagine this type of breathing, think about the way a newborn baby breathes while asleep: slowly and rhythmically. The diaphragm is a dome-shaped muscle that sits below the lungs, horizontally bisecting the trunk of the body. When you breathe in, your diaphragm contracts and flattens downward, creating a vacuum that draws in air. When you exhale, your diaphragm returns to its dome shape, pushing air out of the body. Abdominal breathing is associated with effective inhalation of oxygen and exhalation of carbon dioxide. Increasing awareness of your breathing so that you engage in more abdominal breathing can reduce feelings of tension and anxiety (Davis, Eshelman, and McKay 2008).

Exercise 10.1.   Identifying Your Way of Breathing

Before making changes to your breathing, it is important to spend a few moments identifying how you currently breathe. Being aware, or being mindful, of your current way of breathing will help you recognize when you do make changes. To do so, follow these steps (adapted from Davis, Eshelman, and McKay 2008).

1. Take your left hand and put it on the middle of your chest. Take your right hand and put it on your abdomen, right around your waistline.

2. Breathe. Notice how it feels as the air comes in through your nose, passes through the back of your throat, and then goes into your lungs.

3. Observe your breath for several minutes, without making an effort to change it. What do you notice?

4. Notice which hand rises more when you are inhaling—the left (on your chest) or the right (on your abdomen).

In the preceding exercise, which hand rose more? If it was the right hand, then congratulations—you have already learned the technique of abdominal breathing! If it was the left hand, then you are likely engaging in shallow chest breathing, as many people do regularly without realizing it. Do not worry; in the following exercise (adapted from Davis, Eshelman, and McKay 2008) we will explain step-by-step how to master abdominal breathing.

Exercise 10.2.   Abdominal Breathing

When learning how to breathe more deeply from the abdomen, it is important that you choose a time and a place when you will not be disturbed. Take some time to think about what position may be best for you. You may want to try sitting or lying down with your legs flat on the ground or with your knees slightly raised. In general, try to breathe through your nose, unless you have reason to believe that you cannot effectively obtain air this way (e.g., you have a stuffy nose). If this is the case, you can breathe through your mouth. Note that an audio version of this exercise is available for download at http://www.newharbinger.com/27664.

1. Take either a seated or a lying position. Put one hand on your abdomen with your thumb at your belly button and the other on your chest.

2. Imagine that your abdomen is a balloon that you are slowly filling with air.

3. Breathe in slowly through your nose. Feel the cool air going through your nasal passages as you inhale.

4. Allow your abdomen to expand, rather than your chest. You should feel the hand on your abdomen being pushed away from your body as your abdomen rises. Let the air flow into your upper chest and down your spine—expanding your sides and lower ribs, filling your diaphragm, back, and lower back, and dropping all the way down into your pelvis. Allow the deep inhalation to push your belly out a little bit.

5. As you breathe in, count silently: 1...2...3...4...5. See whether you can continue to inhale up until the count of five, but don't strain yourself; if you can only make it to the count of two, that's fine.

6. Slowly breathe out through your mouth. Let go of your breath in the reverse order that you brought it in. Drop your lower abs, then your belly. Let your ribs pull in, and, finally, let your chest drop as you fully expel all the air.

7. Breathe in through your nose and count silently: 1...2...3...4...5.

8. Slowly breathe out through your mouth.

9. Take five more of these breaths, allowing yourself to experience the feelings of relaxation that accompany this kind of breathing.

As you work on this skill, it is helpful to practice it at the same time and place, on a daily basis. (Consistency is useful when you are learning something new.)

There are many more types of breathing exercises that may be helpful to you. Please see the "Further Reading" section at the end of this book for recommendations.

Exercise 10.3.   The Body Scan

This exercise focuses your attention on your body and the sensations associated with various parts of your body. Like the mindful breathing technique from chapter 6, the body scan strengthens your ability to focus your attention on a single experience over a period of time. In addition, it can draw your attention to emotions you may be experiencing. For example, if you are feeling anxious, you may notice tension in your chest or sensations like butterflies in your stomach. Thus, the body scan helps you better understand body sensations as well as the emotions that may be connected to these sensations. A guided audio version of this exercise is available for download at http://www.newharbinger.com/27664. See back of this book for more details.

To begin, locate a quiet place to perform this exercise. Then settle into a comfortable position, either sitting or lying down. Take several deep breaths and close your eyes.

1. *Focus your attention on your toes and notice any sensations that are there. You may notice pain, a tingling sensation, itchiness, or nothing. Make note of whatever is there. Next, move your attention to the rest of your feet and notice any sensations that are present. As always, do not judge your experience. If you notice your attention wandering, gently bring it back to your feet.*

2. *Slowly working your way up from your feet, notice sensations in the front and back of your lower legs…your knees…the front and back of your upper legs. You may notice tenderness, warmth, coolness, or nothing at all. Make no judgments about what you are experiencing.*

3. *Focus your attention on your lower back. Then slowly move up to your middle back and then upper back. Do you feel tension or pain? Notice any sensations you are experiencing.*

4. *Shift your attention from your upper back to your shoulders and neck, noticing the sensations that are present in this area of your body.*

5. *Focus your attention on your upper arms. Slowly shift your awareness to your elbows, forearms, wrists, hands, and fingers, pausing at each of these locations to observe whatever is present.*

6. *Move your attention to the muscles in your lower abdomen. Does your stomach feel tight or does it feel relaxed? Work your way up toward your stomach and chest, noticing any sensations you feel.*

7. *Turn your attention toward your neck, and slowly work your way up to your chin, your mouth, and the rest of your face. Does your face feel tight or does it feel relaxed? Are your eyes lightly closed or tightly shut? Just observe whatever is present.*

8. *Focus on your head. Are you experiencing any aches, pains, or itches?*

9. *Take several deep breaths before opening your eyes and returning to the external world.*

Imagery

A number of research studies have found that imagining relaxing things or places is an effective means of reducing anxiety. For example, one study examined individuals with high blood pressure—a physical symptom of anxiety—and found that imagery techniques significantly decreased blood pressure over an eight-week period (Crowther 1983). Another study compared test anxiety in two groups of college students: those who were taught to use imagery as a source of relaxation and those who were not (Sapp 1994). Results indicated that use of imagery significantly reduced students' levels of worry and improved their performance on tests.

Exercise 10.4. Visualization: A Beach Scene

Find a comfortable, quiet location in which to do the following exercise. You may find it helpful to lie down, but you can also remain sitting as long as you are comfortable. (If you'd like to listen to a guided version of this meditation, one is available for download at http://www.newharbinger .com/27664.) When you are settled, close your eyes and take several long, deep breaths. Notice the cool air coming in and the warm air going out. Bring your attention to your breathing for a few moments and let yourself become more and more comfortable sitting or lying where you are.

Imagine that you are approaching a beautiful, sunny beach on a warm summer's day. Perhaps this beach is one you have been to before, or perhaps it is one that you are imagining for the first time. You come to the top of a high, wooden stairway that leads to the beach and you begin to walk down it. You have no shoes on, and your bare feet feel the warm, wooden, weather-beaten steps. As you slowly walk down the steps, you feel the tension in your body melting away. You look down the stairs and notice how white the sand is. When you reach the last step, you put your bare feet in the warm sand and feel it between your toes. You dig your foot into the sand and feel the cool sand underneath mixing with the warm sand from above. The sand easily slips through your toes, and you gently wiggle your foot, burrowing it deeper into the sand.

You then start to walk across the sand toward the water. You look to your right and to your left, and it seems as if the bright white sand goes on forever in both directions. The beach is mostly empty, with just the occasional colored umbrella dotting the landscape.

You look toward the water and observe the clear, blue color of the ocean. You see the white crests of the waves gently lapping the shore. You also hear the gentle, rhythmic sound of the waves, and you close your eyes to concentrate on it. As you approach the water, the salty smell of the ocean air intensifies and you take in a deep breath, noticing more tension leaving your body.

You finally reach the water's edge, and you pause there for a moment. You lift your face toward the sun and feel it radiating down upon you, warming you and bringing a feeling of relaxation throughout your body. You put your feet into the cool water and feel the waves gently gliding over your feet. As the waves come in and go out, you feel your feet sink deeper into the cool sand. The cool water feels comforting and relaxing. You gaze out at the expanse of ocean in front of you; there is nothing as far as the eye can see except brilliant blue water. You notice a group of seagulls flying overhead and you hear their soft cries. Occasionally one of them swoops down toward the water and then slowly flies back up into the bright, blue, cloudless sky.

You close your eyes again and allow yourself to take in all the sensations: the warm sun on your face and chest, the salty smell of the ocean air, the sound of the waves and the faint cries of the seagulls, the feel of your feet in the sand and the cool water lapping over them with each wave, in and out. You take several deep breaths and allow the last of the tension to leave your body. You are now feeling fully relaxed and refreshed. Stay by the water's edge experiencing all the sensations of the beach for as long as you like; there is no rush, because you have nowhere to be.

When you feel ready, bring your attention back to the present moment and gently open your eyes. You should feel relaxed and refreshed after your walk at the beach.

Conclusion

Avoiding the things that make you anxious only maintains your anxiety and may actually make it worse over time. Therefore, you should make it a goal to expose yourself to the situations that provoke your anxiety. You can use the anxiety-reduction strategies introduced in this chapter (mindfulness, abdominal breathing, and imagery) while exposing yourself to anxiety-provoking situations or use them in a more general way—to help you fall asleep, for example, or reduce your tension before an important job interview. Depending on how severe your anxiety is, you may benefit from working with a mental health practitioner who can help you design appropriate exposure activities and master anxiety-reduction techniques.

Chapter Summary:

- Avoiding anxiety-provoking situations may feel helpful in the short term, but it is not an effective strategy in the long term.

- Avoidance maintains anxiety and may make it worse over time.

- It is important to expose yourself to the situations that make you feel anxious.

- Mindfulness is the practice of observing your thoughts, feelings, and experiences in a compassionate, nonjudgmental, accepting way.

- Mindfulness teaches you to focus your thoughts away from the topics that make you anxious and tense.

- Increasing awareness of your breathing so that you engage in more abdominal breathing can reduce feelings of tension and anxiety.

- Imagery is another anxiety-reduction strategy.

PART 5

Finding Support and Creating a Personalized Wellness Plan

The last part of this book discusses ways to involve your family, friends, and professional care providers to help keep you healthy. We start with discussing whom to inform about your bipolar II disorder (BPII) and how to approach this conversation. Then, we introduce specific ways to involve family and friends in your wellness. In chapter 12, we put together everything you've learned in this workbook to create a Personalized Wellness Plan. This is a plan that you develop, with support from your family, friends, and professional care providers, to manage your BPII.

CHAPTER 11

Involving Your Family and Friends

Having a strong support team of family, friends, and/or professional care providers can make it easier to cope with your bipolar II disorder (BPII). Such a team can help you recognize early signs and symptoms of mood episodes, maintain a healthy lifestyle, and lend you valuable emotional and practical support in the midst of a mood episode. In fact, a review of a number of research studies on bipolar disorder found that, in addition to psychotherapy and medication adherence, social support was a significant factor in extending periods of wellness (i.e., increasing the length of time between mood episodes) (Altman et al. 2006). Nevertheless, it is not always easy to decide whom to inform about your bipolar disorder and what types of support you should seek. This chapter will go into detail about how to build a support team.

Whom You Should Tell About Your Disorder

Informing others about your BPII can be a difficult task. Although in recent years—in part thanks to well-known individuals like actress Catherine Zeta-Jones, who disclosed her BPII diagnosis—the stigma around mental illness has decreased, some people still have negative notions about what it means to have bipolar disorder. We believe that most of this negativity comes from a lack of understanding about BPII. The good news is that this is something that you can change by educating your family and friends about BPII.

Informing others about your BPII can be helpful in many ways. First, you may feel a sense of relief that your "secret" is out. Second, when others know about your bipolar disorder, they are more likely to be understanding and tolerant of your mood changes. Finally, they can help you manage your illness so that you don't feel as though you are doing it alone.

However, there can also be negative consequences to disclosing your BPII diagnosis. Some people may think that you are not as trustworthy, responsible, or capable. They may have terrible images of what it means to have BPII and become anxious or nervous around you. Your employer could discriminate against you by not promoting you or by laying you off (although this is illegal under the Americans with Disabilities Act). In short, you should think carefully about whom to tell.

Deciding whom to inform about your BPII is largely a personal choice. It is certainly not necessary to tell everyone in your life about your illness. However, there are probably several people who should know about your BPII, to ensure your safety. These people typically include the following:

- All of your doctors

- Your partner or spouse

- Your adolescent or adult children

- Your closest friends and supporters

Beyond this group, however, use your discretion in informing people about your BPII.

Exercise 11.1. Whom to Tell?

The following general questions should help you determine which people to inform about your BPII. You may want to complete this exercise separately for each person you are thinking about telling your BPII diagnosis to. In that case, write the name of the person at the top.

What would be the potential benefits or positive consequences of this person's knowing that I have BPII? (For example, informing your boss could make things easier for you if you miss days of work due to your illness.)

_____

_____

_____

_____

What are the potential risks or negative consequences of this person's knowing that I have BPII? (For example, could you be risking some aspect of your job by informing a coworker?)

_____

_____

_____

_____

Is this person trustworthy? In other words, is this person likely to tell others about my BPII, or is he or she capable of keeping it confidential?

_____

_____

_____

Will this person judge me for having a mental disorder? (Although you cannot predict a person's attitude on mental illness, certain information can serve as an indicator. For example, perhaps you know that this person suffers from panic attacks or has a family member with schizophrenia, which *might* make him or her more accepting of your BPII.)

_____

_____

_____

How will I feel after I tell this person? Will I most likely feel relieved, or am I likely to regret it?

_____

_____

_____

_____

What would my clinician suggest that I do with regard to telling this person? (We encourage you to speak with your doctor or mental health clinician to get his or her thoughts on disclosure to this particular person. It may also be helpful to speak with a close friend.)

_____

_____

_____

How to Tell Others About Your Disorder

It may be difficult to tell others about your BPII. You may feel anxious or nervous. Here are some suggestions to help make these conversations a little easier.

Calm down. It is completely normal to feel anxious or nervous when telling someone that you have BPII. You may want to review the relaxation techniques in chapter 10 to help minimize your anxiety before having one of these discussions.

Know about your illness. Before sharing with others that you have BPII, be well informed about your illness. This includes having a solid understanding of the signs and symptoms, how BPII differs from the more commonly known type (i.e., bipolar I disorder), and knowledge about how BPII is typically treated. It might be helpful to review chapters 1 and 2.

Be aware of your mood. It is ideal to share information about your illness when you are feeling relatively well, rather than when you are in the midst of depression or hypomania. This is because you are in a better position to objectively discuss your illness when you are feeling well.

Choose your surroundings carefully. Carefully choose the time and place to discuss your BPII diagnosis. Select a time when neither you nor the other person(s) has time constraints so that you can allow for plenty of time to talk. Pick a place that is quiet, with no distractions, such as people who may intrude upon your conversation.

Be prepared for questions. Be prepared to answer questions about your illness with specific information. Many of people's fears surrounding mental illness come from a lack of knowledge, so education is key. Let your family and friends know that your set of mood symptoms has a name: BPII. It will be helpful to describe the specific symptoms that you have experienced and explain how these symptoms make up the episodes of depression and hypomania characteristic of BPII.

Following are some sample answers to questions that family members and friends commonly have.

What Is Bipolar II Disorder?

BPII is a type of mental disorder. It means that I have periods of time when my mood is sad or down, called depression. I also have periods of time when my mood is elevated or happy, called hypomania. BPII is different from bipolar I disorder, which is the type of bipolar disorder people most often think of when they hear the term. People with bipolar I disorder have manic episodes, which can be thought of as more intense periods of hypomania. My down periods may last weeks or months, and my elevated times may last days, weeks, or possibly months. Many people with BPII also suffer from anxiety.

(You may want to have your family member or friend read the vignettes in chapter 4 about Katie, Jack, and Martha for a better idea of how these mood episodes may manifest.)

What Are the Signs and Symptoms?

When my mood is elevated (when I am having a hypomanic episode), I may appear to be in a very good mood, although sometimes I may be irritable instead. I may have more energy and confidence than usual, be more productive and talkative, and engage in behaviors or activities that are unusual for me, such as spending a lot of money or being more social. This good mood should not affect my ability to carry out my daily routine, although you may notice a change in my mood and behaviors.

When I am down, I may appear sad or blue. I may lose interest in things that I used to enjoy, lack energy, feel more tired, have difficulties concentrating, or feel guilty. My sleeping and eating habits may change, too; I may sleep or eat more or less than usual. It's possible that I will experience thoughts that life is not worth living or even attempt suicide. All of these symptoms will make it difficult for me to engage in my daily routine.

(If it applies to you, this may be an appropriate juncture to discuss your completed exercise 4.2, "Checklist: Ways to Stay Safe from Suicide.")

What Are the Causes of BPII?

BPII is a biological illness, and it is associated with structural and functional abnormalities in the brain. Scientists know that the disorder is caused, at least in part, by cells in the brain, called neurons, communicating ineffectively with each other through their chemical messengers, which are called neurotransmitters. It is also likely that stress is involved in some way, although stress alone cannot cause the disorder—a person must already have a biological predisposition toward it. However, because the brain is the most complex of all the organs, there is still a lot that is not understood about the causes of BPII, and scientists continue to work on it.

Does BPII Run in Families?

BPII has a very strong genetic basis. There is an average tenfold increased risk of developing BPII among adult relatives of individuals with bipolar I or II disorder (APA 2013). About 25 percent of first-degree relatives of people with BPII will develop some sort of mood disorder (bipolar I or II, depression, or dysthymia, which is a low-grade, chronic type of depression) (Miklowitz 2010). However, there is no way to reliably predict whether the child of someone with BPII will develop BPII or a different disorder.

What Is the Treatment for BPII?

Typical treatments for BPII include psychiatric medication as well as psychotherapy. There are three main classes of medication used to treat BPII: mood stabilizers (e.g., lithium), antidepressants (e.g., Prozac), and atypical antipsychotics (e.g., Abilify), and many people with BPII take more than one medication. In addition, several different types of psychotherapy, or "talk therapy," are used to treat BPII (you may suggest that your family member or friend read chapter 2 to learn about treatments for BPII). Many people with BPII benefit most from psychiatric medication combined with psychotherapy.

Practice Acceptance

Your family and friends are more likely to accept your illness if *you* demonstrate acceptance of it. Remember that practicing acceptance of your BPII does not mean that you necessarily like or enjoy having BPII; it means recognizing that you have an illness so that you can be proactive about monitoring and managing it. You may want to review chapter 3, on acceptance and acceptance-based strategies.

Be Confident About Your Illness

Speak about your illness with confidence. What we mean is that you should come across as self-assured in your knowledge and management of BPII. When you converse with others about any topic (whether it's a decision to leave a job, purchase a new car, or have a child), they generally make judgments or appraisals about the particular topic by the *way* you are talking about it. Do you sound knowledgeable and well informed? Or do you appear tentative and unsure? The way you speak about a topic often dictates the way others will feel about the topic as well. For example, let's say that you have just been fired from your job and you are telling your friend about it. There are several ways that you could share this information:

- "Guess what? The absolute worst thing ever just happened to me: I was fired from my job! I don't know what I am going to do. I am so upset. I feel like crying."

- "Guess what? I was just fired from my job. But I will collect unemployment and find a much better job, so I think everything has turned out for the best."

- "Guess what? I was just fired from my job. I am so mad about it! It's not fair. I am going to write a nasty letter to my boss and try to get him fired."

Your friend will likely make a judgment about your news based on your reaction and the way you discuss it. If you respond with sadness to being fired, he or she will feel sad too; if you indicate you are comfortable with the situation, he or she will feel comfortable too; if you respond with anger, he or she will feel angry too.

In a similar way, you can affect people's reaction to your BPII diagnosis by the way in which you talk about it. For this reason, we recommend that you speak of your diagnosis with confidence and in a matter-of-fact manner, as if telling any other fact about who you are. This is a helpful way of talking about your diagnosis because it suggests that you understand your illness and are confident that you can manage it, and that therefore the other person should be too. In addition, it suggests that you have accepted the diagnosis, at least in part, and therefore the other person should too. Sometimes you may not feel confident about your management or acceptance of your illness, but you can still discuss it in a self-assured manner. Indeed, the saying "Fake it until you make it" may apply during these times. Keep in mind that this does not guarantee that the other person will take the same approach to your illness that you are trying to convey; however, it does increase the likelihood that this will happen.

Know How Others Can Support You

Your family and friends may not always know the most helpful ways to support you. Encourage them to learn about BPII and its treatment. It may be helpful for them to read this book and especially some of your responses to the exercises throughout this book. In addition, it's important to provide them with concrete examples of how they may be able to help and support you, such as the following:

- Recognizing your early warning signs of depression and hypomania

- Assisting you in finding appropriate mental health clinicians or support groups

- Attending one of your mental health appointments (Most mental health clinicians are happy to have supportive family members and friends accompany clients.)

- Helping you file insurance claims

- Reminding you to take your medications

- Reminding you to practice the skills you've learned in this book

- Checking in with you regarding your mood on a regular basis

- Helping you create your Personalized Wellness Plan (discussed in chapter 12)

- Calling, e-mailing, or texting you during difficult times so that you know they are thinking of you

- Planning activities for you to do together as a distraction from depressed moods

- Helping with household chores, such as cleaning, cooking, or grocery shopping, when needed

- Helping with child care when needed

Define How Much Support You Would Like, and What Kind

It is important to identify your personal preferences for support and outline reasonable levels of involvement for members of your support team. For example, perhaps you would like your mother to remind you to take your medications and to accompany you to psychiatrist visits. However, you would prefer that your brother not get involved with those things, but instead provide you with distractions, like dinner or a movie, when you feel depressed. You should specifically communicate your preferences to each member of your support team. It is important to set expectations and boundaries with them so that you don't feel as if they are either too involved or not involved enough. It is best to have these conversations when you are feeling well, rather than in the midst of a crisis.

Inform Your Support Team of When You Would Like Them to Intervene

You are likely to become annoyed if members of your support team nag you every time you seem either slightly down or excited about something. So it is important to discuss with your support team appropriate intervention points. For example, you may want them to gently inform you if they start to notice your early warning signs of depression or hypomania—if you're isolating yourself, for example, or sleeping less. As you know, the sooner you catch symptoms, the easier they are to control; however, you also don't want your support team to overreact to every small mood or behavioral change. Including supportive friends and family members in your Personalized Wellness Plan (discussed in chapter 12) will help them know when it is best to help you.

How to Handle Difficult Reactions

Conversations in which you disclose and discuss your BPII may not always go as well as you had hoped. Perhaps the other person will feel hurt that you didn't share this information at an earlier time. Perhaps he or she will treat you differently (e.g., rejecting or stigmatizing you) because of your illness. If telling someone about your BPII is met with a negative reaction, resist the urge to express anger or resentment. Here are a few ways you might respond.

> "I am sad (or disappointed) that you feel this way. I will not discuss this topic any further today, but please come to me in the future with any questions or concerns. I will be happy to talk to you more about it."

"I was not expecting this response. Is there any more information I can provide that will make you feel more comfortable with this news?"

"I know that this is difficult news to hear and digest. I will give you some time to think about it all."

"I can imagine that this is hard to hear. I would probably feel the same way if I were in your shoes. My goal is to make you as comfortable as possible with this news, so please let me know if there is anything I can do to help with this process."

Notice that all of these statements begin with "I" rather than "you." This is a purposeful communication strategy. Using "I-statements" rather than "you-statements" helps avoid conflict, because such statements indicate ownership of your feelings rather than implying that they are caused by another person. The other person is less likely to become angry or defensive when you use "I-statements."

Support Groups

Although family and friends can provide love and valuable support, they may have trouble relating to your experiences at times, if they don't suffer from bipolar disorder themselves. Others who suffer from bipolar disorder can provide empathy and understanding in ways that those without the illness cannot. Therefore, support groups can be an extremely beneficial resource. Although it may seem intimidating or anxiety provoking to think about discussing such a personal matter with strangers, you will get to know these people over time, and they can become invaluable members of your support team.

Here are some potential benefits of joining a support group:

1. You can connect with others who share your emotions and experiences.

2. You have a place to discuss the frustrations of having bipolar disorder.

3. You can gain new information about medications or therapies.

4. You can learn communication strategies for disclosing and discussing your illness.

5. You may learn about different clinicians in your area.

6. You may find that you develop greater acceptance of your illness by being around others with the same diagnosis.

7. Some support groups feature speakers or expert panels on bipolar disorder.

8. Members of the support group can help you recognize when you are showing early warning signs of a mood episode.

9. You may develop more motivation to follow your treatment plan.

10. You may make new friends.

You are not likely to find a support group that is strictly for people with BPII; most groups include people with both types of bipolar disorder, and some groups even include individuals with other types of mental illness, such as major depression. Nevertheless, these groups can still be beneficial, because many of the symptoms you have and the situations you face are likely shared by at least some of the other group members. Some support groups are run by a facilitator with a degree in psychology, counseling, nursing, medicine, or social work. Other groups are run not by a professional, but by a member or members of the support group. When contacting support groups, you may want to inquire about the leadership of that particular group.

To find out about support groups in your area, contact the following organizations, which sponsor support groups in many cities and towns in the United States:

Depression and Bipolar Support Alliance (DBSA), 1-800-826-3632 or www.dbsalliance.org

Mental Health America (MHA), 1-800-969-6642 or www.mentalhealthamerica.net

National Alliance on Mental Illness (NAMI), 1-800-950-NAMI or www.nami.org

Psychiatrists, psychologists, social workers, and other mental health clinicians may also have information about local support groups. Hopefully, this chapter helped you recognize how having a strong support team can make it easier to cope with your BPII. We hope that you feel more comfortable in your decisions about whom to disclose your diagnosis to and how to discuss it.

Chapter Summary:

- A support team can help you recognize early signs and symptoms of mood episodes, maintain a healthy lifestyle, and lend you valuable emotional and practical support in the midst of depression or hypomania.

- Informing others about your illness can be anxiety provoking, but it can also be very helpful.

- Before disclosing your diagnosis or discussing it with others, it can be helpful to have a good working knowledge of BPII, and to be prepared to answer questions about it.

- Communicate the specific ways in which you would like members of your team to support you. Let them know the extent to which you want them involved and appropriate times to intervene.

- "I-statements" can be a useful communication strategy.

- Support groups can be a valuable resource and extension of your support team.

CHAPTER 12

Putting It All Together to Create a Personalized Wellness Plan

This last chapter focuses on putting together everything you have learned in this book to create a Personalized Wellness Plan. This is a plan that you develop, with support from your family, friends, and/or professional care providers, to manage your bipolar II disorder (BPII). There are five steps to drawing up and implementing your Personalized Wellness Plan, and each step relies on certain parts of this book. Thus, it will be helpful to review certain chapters as you put together your plan—for example, chapter 11 ("Involving Your Family and Friends"), because your family members, friends, and professional care providers can help you with both creating and implementing your plan.

Step 1: Assess Your Wellness

The first step to coming up with any plan is typically to do an assessment, which helps you understand your strengths and weaknesses. Everyone has strengths, or things that they are good at, as well as weaknesses, areas that they could improve upon. This is particularly true in the management of BPII. In chapter 1, we discussed the different symptoms associated with BPII (the depressive symptoms are further explored and defined in chapter 4; hypomanic symptoms, in chapter 7). The following exercise will help you learn more about your particular symptoms.

Exercise 12.1a. Assessing Your Strengths in Managing Bipolar II Disorder

Think about your strengths in handling your particular symptoms of BPII. In the following table, place a check mark next to those symptoms that are easier rather than harder for you to manage. If you do not experience a symptom, do not place a check mark next to it. In the right-hand column, explain why the symptoms that you checked may be easier than other symptoms to manage.

(√)	Depressive Symptoms	Why?
	Loss/gain of appetite	
	Insomnia/hypersomnia	
	Restlessness/agitation	
	Feeling very slowed down	
	Fatigue/loss of energy	
	Feelings of worthlessness or guilt	
	Trouble concentrating/difficulty making decisions	
	Thoughts of death/suicidal ideation	
(√)	Hypomanic Symptoms	Why?
	Abnormally high self-esteem	
	A decreased need for sleep	
	Feeling more talkative than usual	
	Racing thoughts/more ideas than usual	
	Distractibility	
	An increase in goal-directed behavior	
	Involvement in pleasurable activities with high likelihood of negative consequences	

Exercise 12.1b. Assessing Areas You Could Improve Upon in Managing Bipolar II Disorder

Think about your difficulties in handling your particular symptoms of BPII. In the following table, place a check mark next to those symptoms that are harder rather than easier for you to manage. If you do not experience a symptom, do not place a check mark next to it. In the right-hand column, explain why the symptoms that you checked may be harder than other symptoms to manage.

(√)	Depressive Symptoms	Why?
	Loss/gain of appetite	
	Insomnia/hypersomnia	
	Restlessness/agitation	
	Feeling very slowed down	
	Fatigue/loss of energy	
	Feelings of worthlessness or guilt	
	Trouble concentrating/difficulty making decisions	
	Thoughts of death/suicidal ideation	
(√)	Hypomanic Symptoms	Why?
	Abnormally high self-esteem	
	A decreased need for sleep	
	Feeling more talkative than usual	
	Racing thoughts/more ideas than usual	
	Distractibility	
	An increase in goal-directed behavior	
	Involvement in pleasurable activities with high likelihood of negative consequences	

Make sure that you have checked each symptom in the previous two exercises that applies to you, so that you are essentially categorizing each symptom as either "easier" or "harder." You may find it helpful to refer to the symptoms you identified in exercise 4.1, "Self-Test: Symptoms of Depression," and exercise 7.1, "Your Specific Symptoms of Hypomania."

Step 2: Capitalize on Your Strengths

In exercise 12.1a, you identified areas of managing your bipolar disorder that are easier for you and why. In this next step, you will seek to understand *why* it is easier for you to manage certain aspects of your BPII. For example, perhaps you experience these symptoms often, and, therefore, you have developed a strong set of skills or strategies for managing them.

Exercise 12.2.   Building on Your Strengths

In the following table, try to *operationalize*, or define more clearly and specifically, how you are successfully managing each symptom that you identified in exercise 12.1a, "Assessing Your Strengths in Managing Bipolar II Disorder." It may be helpful to review chapters 5 and 6, because these chapters discuss strategies for managing depression, as well as chapter 8, which discusses strategies for managing hypomania. You could even borrow some anxiety-management skills from chapter 10, because mindfulness and relaxation skills can also be helpful for managing depression and hypomania. Together, these chapters can give you tips on how to operationalize what you are doing well in managing your BPII. After you operationalize what you are doing well, try to identify a specific goal that could be useful in continuing to manage that symptom well. You will notice that the first two columns in the table can be copied from exercise 12.1a. We also provide two examples for each kind of symptom.

Symptom I Manage Well	Why?	Operationalize It	Goal
Depressive Symptoms			
Example: *Thoughts of suicide*	*I do not experience this symptom often.*	*I have a good network of friends who support me and whom I talk to if I have such thoughts.*	*Continue to work on maintaining my friendships.*
Example: *Feeling slowed down*	*I force myself to do things.*	*I keep a good schedule of activities.*	*Continue to keep a busy/ active schedule.*

Hypomanic Symptoms			
Example: *Decreased need for sleep*	*I make sure that I get enough sleep even if I don't feel as if I need it.*	*I make myself go to bed at 11:00 p.m. and get out of bed at 7:00 a.m.*	*Continue to keep a regular sleep schedule.*
Example: *Increase in goal-directed behavior*	*Because I keep myself busy normally, I do not have time to do extra activities even when hypomanic.*	*I keep a rigorous, but balanced schedule of activities (e.g., playing basketball, attending painting class).*	*Continue to keep a rigorous and balanced schedule of activities.*

Step 3: Build Up Your Areas That You Could Improve Upon

Everyone has areas that they can improve upon. In fact, an important strength is knowing what these areas are, because this puts you in a better position to manage your BPII. Thus, the next step in building your Personalized Wellness Plan is operationalizing the areas in which you have more difficulty managing your symptoms (which you identified in exercise 12.1b). This is identical to step 2, except now you are creating goals for the symptoms that are more difficult for you to manage. Thus, the same chapters (i.e., chapters 5, 6, 8, and 10) are likely to be helpful for the following exercise. This step is challenging, so before you begin the exercise, carefully review the examples provided to guide you.

Exercise 12.3. Building Up Your Areas That You Could Improve Upon

Symptom I Do Not Manage Well	Why?	Operationalize It	Goal
Depressive Symptoms			
Example: *Increase in appetite*	*I eat much more when I am depressed.*	*I am sad, so I am looking for ways to "fill myself up" or feel better.*	*Distract myself from the urge to eat by doing something else, such as calling a friend or going for a walk.*
Example: *Feelings of worthlessness*	*I think that everyone is better than me.*	*I no longer see my strengths and I focus on my faults.*	*Remind myself of my strengths, or visit someone who can help me do this.*

Hypomanic Symptoms

Example: *Abnormal self-esteem*	*I believe that I am smarter than everyone else at work.*	*I lose sight of what's actually real and create my own reality.*	*Monitor my thoughts daily for hyperpositive thinking and check in with my partner about these thoughts.*
Example: *Distractibility*	*I cannot focus on any one thing at a time.*	*I have difficulty completing tasks at work.*	*Modify my schedule to do less, make a detailed plan for each item that I want to complete, and check in with my boss about each item.*

Step 4: Create Your Personalized Wellness Plan

Now that you have identified your strengths, areas of improvement, and associated goals, you can put all this together to create a Personalized Wellness Plan (exercise 12.4). This plan is to serve as a *contract*, or a binding agreement, between your healthy self (i.e., you when you are not experiencing many symptoms) and your unhealthy self (i.e., you when you are experiencing many symptoms). This is important, because when you are not feeling well (or conversely, when you are feeling very well), you may not always think that you need to stick to a plan, and you may lack the motivation to follow through with the plan. Thus, this contract reminds you that you promised yourself (and your friends, family, and/or professional care providers) that you would do these things when you were feeling unwell.

The first section of your Personalized Wellness Plan identifies at least three to five people to compose your support team. These people may be friends, family, professional care providers, spiritual leaders, or anyone else who can either help you with specific goals (to come in sections 4 and 5) or just support you in following through with your plan. Hopefully, you have already identified these people from your work in chapter 11. Each of these people will sign your plan and receive a copy of it.

Example Personalized Wellness Plan Section 1

1. My Support Team		
Name	Role/Relationship	Contact Information
Mom	*My mom*	*(phone number and/or address)*
Joe	*My friend*	*(phone number and/or address)*
Dr. Sands	*My therapist*	*(phone number and/or address)*
Dr. Smith	*My psychiatrist*	*(phone number and/or address)*
Rev. Walters	*My spiritual mentor*	*(phone number and/or address)*

The second section of your Personalized Wellness Plan identifies your early, or mild, signs of depression and hypomania. The third section identifies the more severe symptoms of depression or hypomania that typically follow your early signs. You may remember doing these exercises in chapters 4 (for depression) and 7 (for hypomania). Thus, it may be helpful to review those exercises when completing these sections of your plan. These sections are very important, because they will help in monitoring your BPII so that you catch symptoms and take appropriate action before the symptoms become too severe. For example, if you know that you tend to eat more pizza just before becoming depressed (because your appetite is increasing or your food cravings are becoming worse), you can take action, when you find yourself eating more pizza, to prevent the depression from getting worse. These sections of the plan are also very important to review with your support team so that the members of your support team can help you monitor and manage your illness.

Example Personalized Wellness Plan Sections 2 and 3

2. Identifying Early Signs of a Mood Episode	
Depressive Symptom	**How Does This Symptom Affect Me?**
I sleep thirty minutes longer than usual.	*I am late to work.*
I have increased cravings for unhealthy foods.	*I begin cooking less and ordering in for food. I begin gaining weight.*
I feel more gloomy and sad.	*I call my friends less often and isolate.*
I am more tired during the day.	*I exercise less often and get less done.*
I have less interest in doing things.	*I isolate more from my friends and family.*
Hypomanic Symptom	**How Does This Symptom Affect Me?**
I feel more self-confident.	*I begin to wear more colorful clothing and people say that I "have an ego."*
I have more energy than usual.	*I start too many projects and then have difficulty completing them.*
I am more talkative than usual.	*I interrupt other people and talk over them.*
I have difficulty concentrating.	*I no longer enjoy reading (usually a good coping strategy for me) and my job is harder to do.*
I feel more irritable.	*I have more difficulty interacting with my friends and coworkers.*

3. Identifying Later Signs of a Mood Episode	
Depressive Symptom	**How Does This Symptom Affect Me?**
I have difficulty getting out of bed.	I am consistently very late to work; my boss becomes upset with me.
I binge eat.	I gain weight and have negative thoughts about myself.
I am in a sad mood nearly all the time.	I do not see my friends and family.
I am tired all day.	I stop exercising and am less productive at work such that it begins to cause problems.
I have no interest in doing things.	I do not want to do basic tasks, such as showering, cooking, and returning e-mails.
Hypomanic Symptom	**How Does This Symptom Affect Me?**
I am in an elevated mood.	I make inappropriate jokes and think that I do not need to work.
I am overly energetic.	I find myself up late at night cleaning the house and not feeling tired.
I do not take my medications.	My elevated mood gets worse.
I am unable to concentrate.	I am not able to do my work.
I have anger, or high-energy irritability.	I say unpleasant or mean things and upset others.

The fourth section of your Personalized Wellness Plan indicates the specific goals you have identified (in exercises 12.2 and 12.3) to take action against your depression and hypomania. We have gone ahead and listed some strategies that might be helpful for you in this section (see exercise 12.4 or the following example). Place a check mark next to each of the strategies and/or coping skills that you think would help you, then write in the name of the person whose help you might want with each one in the far right-hand column. For example, perhaps you are willing to have your mom help you create your daily schedule, but you would prefer your friend to talk to you about taking your medications. Knowing who can help you and when is a very important part of your plan. There are several lines marked "Other." These are for you to write in specific goals that you identified in exercises 12.2 and 12.3 to help you manage your bipolar symptoms. Remember to build upon your strengths, so look carefully at exercise 12.2 to see what you are already doing to manage your bipolar symptoms.

Example Personalized Wellness Plan Section 4

4a. Taking Action Against My Depressive Symptoms		
(√)	Things to Do	Who Can Help?
√	Contact my psychiatrist.	Dr. Smith
√	Contact my therapist.	Dr. Sands
√	Contact my support person.	Mom
√	Maintain a regular schedule of activities.	Mom
√	Maintain a regular sleep schedule.	Mom, Joe
√	Evaluate my thinking, or practice cognitive restructuring.	Dr. Smith
√	Take my medications.	Dr. Sands, Mom
√	Monitor my mood.	Dr. Sands, Joe
√	Reduce my alcohol intake, or stop it.	Dr. Smith
√	Increase my daily exercise.	Rev. Walters

√	Work on my anti-craving strategies for food.	Joe
√	Make a plan to complete an activity.	Joe, Mom
√	Watch a movie, or identify distracting activities.	Joe
√	Other: *Schedule at least three activities a week with a friend.*	Mom
√	Other: *Get a ride to work with a coworker.*	Mom
√	Other: *Cook at least four meals a week.*	Joe, Rev. Walters
√	Other: *Keep a diary or journal.*	
√	Other:	

4b. Taking Action Against My Hypomanic Symptoms

√	**Things to Do**	**Who Can Help?**
√	Talk to me about my hypomanic symptoms.	*Drs. Smith and Sands*
√	Take my medications.	*Dr. Smith*
√	Talk to me about reducing my activities.	*Dr. Sands, Mom*
√	Increase my daily structure.	*Dr. Sands, Mom*
√	Maintain a regular sleep schedule.	*Dr. Sands, Joe*

√	Evaluate my thinking, or practice cognitive restructuring.	*Rev. Walters*
√	Take away my credit cards.	*Dr. Sands, Mom*
√	Encourage me to do self-soothing or relaxing activities.	*Drs. Smith/Sands*
√	Remind me not to talk to people when I am angry or irritable.	*Rev. Walters*
√	Do not start any new projects.	*Mom, Joe*
√	Make a plan to complete my current activities and to focus.	*Rev. Walters, Dr. Sands*
√	Reduce my stimulating activities.	*Dr. Sands*
√	Other: *Count to three before speaking.*	Mom
√	Other: *Run my ideas by at least one other person before acting.*	Mom
√	Other: *Start three less projects at work a week.*	*Joe*
√	Other: *Do not start cleaning the house after 9:00 p.m.*	Mom
	Other:	

The next section of the Personalized Wellness Plan may not pertain to everyone, but it could be vital for some. In this section, you make a specific plan to help you manage your suicidal thoughts. If you have never had thoughts that your life is not worth living, we still encourage you to complete this section. In short, it is better to have a plan in place in case you develop such thoughts. Identify whom you would want to tell if you were having suicidal thoughts. Enter their name and phone numbers in your plan. Remember that each member of your support team will receive a copy of this plan, so it is very helpful to have every piece of important information in this plan. Similarly, identify the emergency room (ER) that you would want to be transported to in the case of emergency with your BPII. It does not have to be the closest ER, but it should be one to which you can be transported quickly.

Example Personalized Wellness Plan Section 5

5. Managing My Suicidal Thoughts	
√	Contact the following people should I ever have strong suicidal thoughts:
√	My psychiatrist: *Dr. Smith (phone number)*
√	My therapist: *Dr. Sands (phone number)*
√	My family: *Mom (phone number)*
√	My friend(s): *Joe (phone number)*
√	Other: *Rev. Walters (phone number)*
√	Keep myself safe or go to local ER, if I am unable to.
√	Other: *Have someone remind me of my positive thoughts.*
√	Other: *Spend time with my pets.*
√	Other: *Have someone help me take my medications.*
√	Other: *Reread my journal.*
	Other:

The last section of the Personalized Wellness Plan is for you and each member of your support team to sign. This is to remind you that you are making a contract with yourself, as well as with your support team, to do the things that you have identified to manage your BPII. It is also a reminder that you do have support. Indeed, the signatures of the members of your support team indicate that you have people who are committed to helping you stay well. Each person who signs the plan should receive a copy of it and keep it in an easily accessible place.

Exercise 12.4 offers a blank Personalized Wellness Plan. An electronic version is available at http://www.newharbinger.com/27664 (see the back of this book for more information). You may want to start thinking about your plan on your own, but seek help from your support team in filling it out, because we suspect that you will find their feedback very helpful. *Remember: your Personalized Wellness Plan is your commitment to yourself and others that you will try your best to manage your BPII.*

Exercise 12.4.   Your Contract: Creating Your Personalized Wellness Plan

1. My Support Team		
Name	Role/Relationship	Contact Information

2. Identifying Early Signs of a Mood Episode	
Depressive Symptom	How Does This Symptom Affect Me?
Hypomanic Symptom	How Does This Symptom Affect Me?

3. Identifying Later Signs of a Mood Episode	
Depressive Symptom	How Does This Symptom Affect Me?
Hypomanic Symptom	How Does This Symptom Affect Me?

4a. Taking Action Against My Depressive Symptoms		
(√)	Things to Do	Who Can Help?
	Contact my psychiatrist:	
	Contact my therapist:	
	Contact my support person:	
	Maintain a regular schedule of activities.	
	Maintain a regular sleep schedule.	
	Evaluate my thinking, or practice cognitive restructuring.	
	Take my medications.	
	Monitor my mood.	
	Reduce my alcohol intake, or stop it.	
	Increase my daily exercise.	
	Work on my anti-craving strategies for food.	
	Make a plan to complete an activity.	
	Watch a movie, or identify distracting activities.	
	Other:	
	Other:	
	Other:	
	Other:	
	Other:	

4b. Taking Action Against My Hypomanic Symptoms		
(√)	**Things to Do**	**Who Can Help?**
	Talk to me about my hypomanic symptoms.	
	Take my medications.	
	Talk to me about reducing my activities.	
	Increase my daily structure.	
	Maintain a regular sleep schedule.	
	Evaluate my thinking, or practice cognitive restructuring.	
	Take away my credit cards.	
	Encourage me to do self-soothing or relaxing activities.	
	Remind me not to talk to people when I am angry or irritable.	
	Do not start any new projects.	
	Make a plan to complete my current activities and to focus.	
	Reduce my stimulating activities.	
	Other:	
	Other:	
	Other:	
	Other:	
	Other:	

5. Managing My Suicidal Thoughts	
(√)	**Things to Do**
	Contact the following people should I ever have strong suicidal thoughts:
	My psychiatrist:
	My therapist:
	My family:
	My friend(s):
	Other:
	Keep myself safe or go to local ER, if I am unable to.
	Other:
	Other:
	Other:
	Other:
	Other:

6. Signatures

Signature	Date	Signature	Date
Signature	Date	Signature	Date
Signature	Date	Signature	Date

Step 5: Use and Modify Your Personalized Wellness Plan

The last step in drawing up and implementing your Personalized Wellness Plan is to actually use it! One important way to use it is to keep it with you so that you can regularly monitor your symptoms. Your signs of a mood episode in sections 2 and 3 are particularly important to keep track of on a regular basis.

We recommend that you practice using your Personalized Wellness Plan even when you are feeling healthy by using the strategies and goals that you identified in sections 4 and 5. It is often easier to practice these skills and strategies when you are feeling well, and when you do this, it will be easier for you to use and apply them when you become more ill.

A third way, and perhaps the most important way, to use your Personalized Wellness Plan is to stick to it when your BPII worsens—in other words, when it is the hardest to use it. Your plan is intended to not only keep you safe, but also help you avoid a number of negative outcomes, such as damaging your relationships, developing problems at work, gaining or losing too much weight, or making decisions that you might regret. It is intended to keep you as healthy as possible, even when you are not feeling very well.

Important: If your Personalized Wellness Plan does not help you manage your BPII, then it needs to be modified.

Therefore, our final tip for using your Personalized Wellness Plan is to modify what is not working. For example, you may identify additional skills that you want to add to your plan. Or you may discover that some skills on your plan are not as useful as they once were, are not really helping you, or are just too hard to use when you are not feeling well. In these cases, remove these skills and goals from your plan. Your plan should be feasible. If it is not, then it needs to be reevaluated and modified. It may take several trials and revisions to create a plan that really works for you. Remember that your friends, family, and professional care providers can be very helpful as you create your plan, so continue to seek input from your support team, and always create a final version that you and your team sign off on. This is a contract. If you treat it as such, you will increase the likelihood of successfully managing your illness.

Chapter Summary:

- A Personalized Wellness Plan can help you manage your BPII, especially when you are not feeling well.

- A Personalized Wellness Plan is most likely to be helpful when you incorporate input from people who know you well.

- A Personalized Wellness Plan includes knowing your early signs of depression and hypomania, what you do well in managing your illness, what areas of illness management you need to improve upon, a suicidal-thought action plan, and signatures from you and the members of your support team.

- A Personalized Wellness Plan is a contract between your healthy self and your unhealthy self.

- A Personalized Wellness Plan needs to be followed to be effective, so it must be feasible.

- A Personalized Wellness Plan that is not feasible or helpful must be modified.

Further Reading

Note that some titles are listed under more than one category.

Bipolar Disorder

Fink, C., and J. Kraynak. 2005. *Bipolar Disorder for Dummies*. Hoboken, NJ: Wiley Publishing.

Jamison, K. R. 1995. *An Unquiet Mind*. New York: Random House Digital.

Miklowitz, D. 2010. *The Bipolar Disorder Survival Guide: What You and Your Family Need to Know*. 2nd ed. New York: Guilford Press.

Phelps, J. 2006. *Why Am I Still Depressed? Recognizing and Managing Ups and Downs Of Bipolar II and Soft Bipolar Disorder*. New York: McGraw-Hill.

Ramirez Basco, M. 2006. *The Bipolar Workbook: Tools for Controlling Your Mood Swings*. New York: Guilford Press.

Smith, H. 2010. *Welcome to the Jungle: Everything You Ever Wanted to Know About Bipolar But Were Too Freaked Out to Ask*. San Francisco, CA: Conari Press.

Torrey, E. F., and M. B. Knable. 2002. *Surviving Manic Depression: A Manual on Bipolar Disorder for Patients, Families, and Providers*. New York: Basic Books.

Van Dijk, S. 2009. *The Dialectical Behavior Therapy Skills Workbook for Bipolar Disorder: Using DBT to Regain Control of Your Emotions and Your Life*. Oakland, CA: New Harbinger Publications.

Depression

Burns, D. 1999. *Feeling Good: The New Mood Therapy*. Rev. and updated. New York: Avon Books.

Greenberger, D., and C. Padesky. 1995. *Mind over Mood: Change How You Feel by Changing the Way You Think*. New York: Guilford Press.

Knaus, W. J. 2006. *The Cognitive Behavioral Workbook for Depression*. Oakland, CA: New Harbinger Publications.

McKay, M., M. Davis, and P. Fanning. 2007. *Thoughts and Feelings: Taking Control of Your Moods and Your Life*. Oakland, CA: New Harbinger Publications.

Otto, M., and J.A.J. Smits. 2011. *Exercise for Mood and Anxiety: Proven Strategies for Overcoming Depression and Enhancing Well-Being*. New York: Oxford University Press.

Phelps, J. 2006. *Why Am I Still Depressed? Recognizing and Managing the Ups and Downs of Bipolar II and Soft Bipolar Disorder*. New York: McGraw-Hill.

Strosahl, K. D., and P. J. Robinson. 2008. *The Mindfulness and Acceptance Workbook for Depression*. Oakland, CA: New Harbinger Publications.

Williams, M., J. Teasdale, Z. Segal, and J. Kabat-Zinn. 2007. *The Mindful Way Through Depression: Freeing Yourself from Chronic Unhappiness*. New York: Guilford Press.

Hypomania

Doran, C. 2007. *The Hypomania Handbook: The Challenge of Elevated Mood*. Philadelphia: Lippincott, Williams & Wilkins.

Anxiety and Stress Reduction

Bourne, E. 2011. *The Anxiety and Phobia Workbook*. 5th ed. Oakland, CA: New Harbinger Publications.

Chapman, A. L., K. L. Gratz, and M. Tull. 2011. *The Dialectical Behavior Therapy Skills Workbook for Anxiety: Breaking Free from Worry, Panic, PTSD, and Other Anxiety Symptoms*. Oakland, CA: New Harbinger Publications.

Davis, M., E. Eshelman, and M. McKay. 2008. *The Relaxation and Stress Reduction Workbook.* 6th ed. Oakland, CA: New Harbinger Publications.

Forsyth, J. P., and G. H. Eifert. 2008. *The Mindfulness and Acceptance Workbook for Anxiety: A Guide to Breaking Free from Anxiety, Phobias, and Worry Using Acceptance and Commitment Therapy.* Oakland, CA: New Harbinger Publications.

Stahl, B., and E. Goldstein. 2010. *A Mindfulness-Based Stress Reduction Workbook.* Oakland, CA: New Harbinger Publications.

Wehrenberg, M. 2008. *The 10 Best-Ever Anxiety Management Techniques: Understanding How Your Brain Makes You Anxious and What You Can Do to Change It.* New York: W. W. Norton.

Cognitive Behavioral Therapy (CBT)

Burns, D. 1999. *Feeling Good: The New Mood Therapy.* Rev. and updated. New York: Avon Books.

Greenberger, D., and C. Padesky. 1995. *Mind over Mood: Change How You Feel by Changing the Way You Think.* New York: Guilford Press.

Knaus, W. J. 2006. *The Cognitive Behavioral Workbook for Depression.* Oakland, CA: New Harbinger Publications.

Ramirez Basco, M. 2006. *The Bipolar Workbook: Tools for Controlling Your Mood Swings.* New York: Guilford Press.

Dialectical Behavior Therapy (DBT)

Chapman, A. L., K. L. Gratz, and M. Tull. 2011. *The Dialectical Behavior Therapy Skills Workbook for Anxiety: Breaking Free from Worry, Panic, PTSD, and Other Anxiety Symptoms.* Oakland, CA: New Harbinger Publications.

Linehan, M. M. 1993. *Skills Training Manual for Treating Borderline Personality Disorder.* New York: Guilford Press.

Marra, T. 2004. *Depressed and Anxious: The Dialectical Behavior Therapy Workbook for Overcoming Depression and Anxiety.* Oakland, CA: New Harbinger Publications.

McKay, M., J. C. Wood, and J. Brantley. 2007. *The Dialectical Behavior Therapy Skills Workbook: Practical DBT Exercises for Learning Mindfulness, Interpersonal Effectiveness, Emotion Regulation, and Distress Tolerance.* Oakland, CA: New Harbinger Publications.

Spradlin, S. 2003. *Don't Let Your Emotions Run Your Life: How Dialectical Behavior Therapy Can Put You in Control*. Oakland, CA: New Harbinger Publications.

Van Dijk, S. 2009. *The Dialectical Behavior Therapy Skills Workbook for Bipolar Disorder: Using DBT to Regain Control of Your Emotions and Your Life*. Oakland, CA: New Harbinger Publications.

Mindfulness

Alidina, S. 2010. *Mindfulness for Dummies*. Chichester, West Sussex, England: John Wiley & Sons.

Kabat-Zinn, J. 1990. *Full Catastrophe Living: Using the Wisdom of Your Body and Mind to Face Stress, Pain, and Illness*. New York: Random House.

Kabat-Zinn, J. 1994. *Wherever You Go, There You Are: Mindfulness Meditation in Everyday Life*. New York: Hyperion.

Kabat-Zinn, J. 2012. *Mindfulness for Beginners*. Boulder, CO: Sounds True.

Stahl, B., and E. Goldstein. 2010. *A Mindfulness-Based Stress Reduction Workbook*. Oakland, CA: New Harbinger Publications.

Strosahl, K. D., and P. J. Robinson. 2008. *The Mindfulness and Acceptance Workbook for Depression*. Oakland, CA: New Harbinger Publications.

Williams, M., J. Teasdale, Z. Segal, and J. Kabat-Zinn. 2007. *The Mindful Way Through Depression: Freeing Yourself from Chronic Unhappiness*. New York: Guilford Press.

Exercise and Nutrition

Beck, J. S. 2007. *The Beck Diet Solution: Train Your Brain to Think Like a Thin Person*. Birmingham, AL: Oxmoor House.

Brownell, K. 2004. *The LEARN Program for Weight Management*. Euless, TX: American Health Publishing.

Otto, M., and J.A.J. Smits. 2011. *Exercise for Mood and Anxiety: Proven Strategies for Overcoming Depression and Enhancing Well-Being*. New York: Oxford University Press.

Sleep

Carney, C., and R. Manber. 2009. *Quiet Your Mind and Get to Sleep: Solutions to Insomnia for Those with Depression, Anxiety, or Chronic Pain*. Oakland, CA: New Harbinger Publications.

Jacobs, G. 2009. *Say Good Night to Insomnia*. New York: Holt Paperbacks.

Family Support

Fast, J. A., and J. D. Preston. 2004. *Loving Someone with Bipolar Disorder: Understanding and Helping Your Partner*. Oakland, CA: New Harbinger Publications.

Lowe, C., and B. M. Cohen. 2010. *Living with Someone Who's Living with Bipolar Disorder*. San Francisco: Jossey-Bass.

Miklowitz, D. 2010. *The Bipolar Disorder Survival Guide: What You and Your Family Need to Know*. 2nd ed. New York: Guilford Press.

Torrey, E. F., and M. B. Knable. 2002. *Surviving Manic Depression: A Manual on Bipolar Disorder for Patients, Families, and Providers*. New York: Basic Books.

References

Alloy, L. B., S. Urosevic, L. Y. Abramson, S. Jager-Hyman, R. Nusslock, W. G. Whitehouse, and M. Hogan. 2012. "Progression Along the Bipolar Spectrum: A Longitudinal Study of Predictors of Conversion from Bipolar Spectrum Conditions to Bipolar I and II Disorders." *Journal of Abnormal Psychology* 121 (1): 16–27.

Altman, S., S. Haeri, L. J. Cohen, A. Ten, E. Barron, I. I. Galynker, and K. N. Duhamel. 2006. "Predictors of Relapse in Bipolar Disorder: A Review." *Journal of Psychiatric Practice* 12 (5): 269–82.

APA. 2013. *Diagnostic and Statistical Manual of Mental Disorders.* 5th ed. Washington, DC: American Psychiatric Association.

Baek, J. H., D. Y. Park, J. Choi, J. S. Kim, J. S. Choi, K. Ha, J. S. Kwon, D. Lee, and K. S. Hong. 2011. "Differences Between Bipolar I and Bipolar II Disorders in Clinical Features, Comorbidity, and Family History." *Journal of Affective Disorders* 131 (1-3): 59–67.

Ball, J. R., P. B. Mitchell, J. C. Corry, A. Skillecorn, M. Smith, and G. S. Malhi. 2006. "A Randomized Controlled Trial of Cognitive Therapy for Bipolar Disorder: Focus on Long-Term Change." *Journal of Clinical Psychiatry* 67 (2): 277–86.

Barlow, D. H., L. B. Allen, and M. L. Choate. 2004. "Towards a Unified Treatment for Emotional Disorders." *Behavior Therapy* 35(2): 205–30.

Beck, A. T. 1976. *Cognitive Therapy and the Emotional Disorders.* New York: International Universities Press.

Beck, A. T., A. J. Rush, B. F. Shaw, and G. Emery. 1979. *Cognitive Therapy of Depression.* New York: Guilford Press.

Brugue, E., F. Colom, J. Sanchez-Moreno, N. Cruz, and E. Vieta. 2008. "Depression Subtypes in Bipolar I and II Disorders." *Psychopathology* 41 (2): 111–14.

Burns, D. 1980. *Feeling Good: The New Mood Therapy.* New York: Morrow.

Burns, D. 1999. *Feeling Good: The New Mood Therapy.* Rev. and updated. New York: Avon Books.

Chapman, A. L., K. L. Gratz, and M. Tull. 2011. *The Dialectical Behavior Therapy Skills Workbook for Anxiety: Breaking Free from Worry, Panic, PTSD, and Other Anxiety Symptoms.* Oakland, CA: New Harbinger Publications.

Choi, J., J. H. Baek, J. Noh, J. S. Kim, J. S. Choi, K. Ha, J. S. Kwon, and K. S. Hong. 2011. "Association of Seasonality and Premenstrual Symptoms in Bipolar I and Bipolar II Disorders." *Journal of Affective Disorders* 129 (1-3): 313–16.

Cochran, S. D. 1984. "Preventing Medical Noncompliance in the Outpatient Treatment of Bipolar Affective Disorders." *Journal of Consulting and Clinical Psychology* 52 (5): 873–78.

Colom, F., and E. Vieta. 2006. *Psychoeducation Manual for Bipolar Disorder.* New York: Cambridge University Press.

Colom, F., E. Vieta, A. Martinez-Aran, M. Reinares, J. M. Goikolea, A. Benabarre, et al. 2003. "A Randomized Trial on the Efficacy of Group Psychoeducation in the Prophylaxis of Recurrences in Bipolar Patients Whose Disease Is in Remission." *Archives of General Psychiatry* 60 (4): 402–7.

Crowther, J. H. 1983. "Stress Management Training and Relaxation Imagery in the Treatment of Essential Hypertension." *Journal of Behavioral Medicine* 6 (2): 169–87.

Davis, M., E. R. Eshelman, and M. McKay. 2008. *The Relaxation and Stress Reduction Workbook.* 6th ed. Oakland, CA: New Harbinger Publications.

Deckersbach, T., B. K. Hölzel, L. R. Eisner, J. P. Stange, A. D. Peckham, D. D. Dougherty, S. L. Rauch, S. Lazar, and A. A. Nierenberg. 2012. "Mindfulness-Based Cognitive Therapy for Nonremitted Patients with Bipolar Disorder." *CNS Neuroscience and Therapeutics* 18 (2): 133–41.

Deckersbach, T., R. H. Perlis, W. G. Frankle, S. M. Gray, L. Grandin, D. D. Dougherty, A. A. Nierenberg, and G. S. Sachs. 2004. "Presence of Irritability During Depressive Episodes in Bipolar Disorder." *CNS Spectrums* 9 (3): 227–31.

Dias, R. S., B. Lafer, C. Russo, A. Del Debbio, A. A. Nierenberg, G. S. Sachs, and H. Joffe. 2011. "Longitudinal Follow-up of Bipolar Disorder in Women with Premenstrual Exacerbation: Findings from STEP-BD." *American Journal of Psychiatry* 168 (4): 386–94.

Dobson, K. S. 1989. "A Meta-Analysis of the Efficacy of Cognitive Therapy for Depression." *Journal of Consulting and Clinical Psychology* 57 (3): 414–19.

Ehlers, C. L., E. Frank, and D. J. Kupfer. 1988. "Social Zeitgebers and Biological Rhythms: A Unified Approach to Understanding the Etiology of Depression." *Archives of General Psychiatry* 45 (10): 948–52.

Eisner, L. R., S. Gironde, S. McMurrich, A. Hay, A. D. Peckham, A. T. Peters, A. A. Nierenberg, and T. Deckersbach. 2011. "Enhancing Emotion Regulation in Bipolar Disorder." Poster presented at the 45th annual meeting of the Association for Behavioral and Cognitive Therapies, Toronto, Canada, November.

Elmslie, J. L., J. I. Mann, J. T. Silverstone, S. M. Williams, and S. E. Romans. 2001. "Determinants of Overweight and Obesity in Patients with Bipolar Disorder." *Journal of Clinical Psychiatry* 62 (6): 486–93.

Fava, G. A., C. Ruini, C. Rafanelli, L. Finos, S. Conti, and S. Grandi. 2004. "Six-Year Outcome of Cognitive Behavior Therapy for Prevention of Recurrent Depression." *American Journal of Psychiatry* 161 (10): 1872–76.

Frank, E. 2005. *Treating Bipolar Disorder: A Clinician's Guide to Interpersonal and Social Rhythm Therapy.* New York: Guilford Press.

Frank, E., D. J. Kupfer, M. E. Thase, A. G. Mallinger, H. A. Swartz, A. M. Fagiolini, et al. 2005. "Two-Year Outcomes for Interpersonal and Social Rhythm Therapy in Individuals with Bipolar I Disorder." *Archives of General Psychiatry* 62 (9): 996–1004.

Frank, E., H. A. Swartz, and D. J. Kupfer. 2000. "Interpersonal and Social Rhythm Therapy: Managing the Chaos of Bipolar Disorder." *Biological Psychiatry* 48 (6): 593–604.

Friedman, E., L. Gyulai, M. Bhargava, M. Landen, S. Wisniewski, J. Foris, M. Ostacher, R. Medina, and M. Thase. 2006. "Seasonal Changes in Clinical Status in Bipolar Disorder: A Prospective Study in 1000 STEP-BD Patients." *Acta Psychiatrica Scandinavica* 113 (6): 510–17.

Goldberg, I. 2013. *Goldberg Bipolar Screening Inventory.* Psych Central 1993 [cited April 13 2013]. Available from http://psychcentral.com/quizzes/bipolarquiz.htm.

Goldstein, T. R., D. A. Axelson, B. Birmaher, and D. A. Brent. 2007. "Dialectical Behavior Therapy for Adolescents with Bipolar Disorder: A 1-Year Open Trial." *Journal of the American Academy of Child and Adolescent Psychiatry* 46 (7): 820–30.

Gonda, X., M. Pompili, G. Serafini, F. Montebovi, S. Campi, P. Dome, T. Duleba, P. Girardi, and Z. Rihmer. 2012. "Suicidal Behavior in Bipolar Disorder: Epidemiology, Characteristics and Major Risk Factors." *Journal of Affective Disorders* 143 (1-3): 16–26.

Grandin, L. D., L. B. Alloy, and L. Y. Abramson. 2006. "The Social Zeitgeber Theory, Circadian Rhythms, and Mood Disorders: Review and Evaluation." *Clinical Psychology Review* 26 (6): 679–94.

Ingram, R. E., and D. D. Luxton. 2005. "Vulnerability-Stress Models." In *Development of Psychopathology: A Vulnerability-Stress Perspective,* edited by B. L. Hankin and J.R.Z. Abela, 32–46. Thousand Oaks, CA: Sage Publications.

Johnson, S. L. 2005. "Life Events in Bipolar Disorder: Towards More Specific Models." *Clinical Psychology Review* 25 (8): 1008–27.

Johnson, S. L., A. K. Cueller, C. Ruggero, C. Winett-Perlman, P. Goodnick, R. White, and I. Miller. 2008. "Life Events as Predictors of Mania and Depression in Bipolar I Disorder." *Journal of Abnormal Psychology* 117 (2): 268–77.

Johnson, S. L., and I. Miller. 1997. "Negative Life Events and Time to Recovery from Episodes of Bipolar Disorder." *Journal of Abnormal Psychology* 106 (3): 449–57.

Kabat-Zinn, J. 1990. *Full Catastrophe Living: Using the Wisdom of Your Body and Mind to Face Stress, Pain, and Illness.* New York: Bantam Dell.

———. 1994. *Wherever You Go, There You Are: Mindfulness Meditation in Everyday Life.* New York: Hyperion.

Kabat-Zinn, J., A. O. Massion, J. Kristeller, L. G. Peterson, K. E. Fletcher, L. Pbert, W. R. Lenderking, and S. F. Santorelli. 1992. "Effectiveness of a Meditation-Based Stress Reduction Program in the Treatment of Anxiety Disorders." *American Journal of Psychiatry* 149 (7): 936–43.

Keefe, N. 2009. *Most Memorable Quotes in Boston Sports History*. NESN.com. Available from http://nesn.com/2009/08/most-memorable-quotes-in-boston-sports-history/.

Kessler, R. C., W. T. Chiu, O. Demler, and E. E. Walters. 2005. "Prevalence, Severity, and Comorbidity of 12-Month DSM-IV Disorders in the National Comorbidity Survey Replication." *Archives of General Psychiatry* 62 (6): 617–27.

Kilbourne, A. M., D. L. Rofey, J. F. McCarthy, E. P. Post, D. Welsh, and F. C. Blow. 2007. "Nutrition and Exercise Behavior Among Patients with Bipolar Disorder." *Bipolar Disorders* 9 (5): 443–52.

Kim, D. R., K. A. Czarkowski, and C. N. Epperson. 2011. "The Relationship Between Bipolar Disorder, Seasonality, and Premenstrual Symptoms." *Current Psychiatry Reports* 13 (6): 500–503.

Kutz, I., J. Z. Borysenko, and H. Benson. 1985. "Meditation and Psychotherapy: A Rationale for the Integration of Dynamic Psychotherapy, the Relaxation Response, and Mindfulness Meditation." *American Journal of Psychiatry* 142 (1): 1–8.

Lam, D. H., P. Hayward, E. R. Watkins, K. Wright, and P. Sham. 2005. "Relapse Prevention in Patients with Bipolar Disorder: Cognitive Therapy Outcome After 2 Years." *American Journal of Psychiatry* 162 (2): 324–29.

Lam, D. H., S. Jones, P. Hayward, and J. Bright. 1999. *Cognitive Therapy for Bipolar Disorder: A Therapist's Guide to Concepts, Methods, and Practice*. Chichester, West Sussex, England: John Wiley & Sons.

Lawlor, D. A., and S. W. Hopker. 2001. "The Effectiveness of Exercise as an Intervention in the Management of Depression: Systematic Review and Meta-Regression Analysis of Randomised Controlled Trials." *British Medical Journal* 322 (7289): 763–67.

Linehan, M. M. 1993a. *Cognitive Behavioral Treatment of Borderline Personality Disorder*. New York: Guilford Press.

———. 1993b. *Skills Training Manual for Treating Borderline Personality Disorder*. New York: Guilford Press.

Linehan, M. M., K. A. Comtois, A. M. Murray, M. Z. Brown, R. J. Gallop, H. L. Heard, K. E. Korslund, D. A. Tutek, S. K. Reynolds, and N. Lindenboim. 2006. "Two-Year Randomized Controlled Trial and Follow-up of Dialectical Behavior Therapy vs Therapy by Experts for Suicidal Behaviors and Borderline Personality Disorder." *Archives of General Psychiatry* 63 (7): 757–66.

Linehan, M. M., H. Schmidt, L. A. Dimeff, J. C. Craft, J. Kanter, and K. A. Comtois. 1999. "Dialectical Behavior Therapy for Patients with Borderline Personality Disorder and Drug-Dependence." *American Journal on Addictions* 8 (4): 279–92.

Lynch, T. R., J. Q. Morse, T. Mendelson, and C. J. Robins. 2003. "Dialectical Behavior Therapy for Depressed Older Adults: A Randomized Pilot Study." *American Journal of Geriatric Psychiatry* 11 (1): 33–45.

Ma, S. H., and J. D. Teasdale. 2004. "Mindfulness-Based Cognitive Therapy for Depression: Replication and Exploration of Differential Relapse Prevention Effects." *Journal of Consulting and Clinical Psychology* 72 (1): 31–40.

Marsh, W. K., T. A. Ketter, and N. L. Rasgon. 2009. "Increased Depressive Symptoms in Menopausal Age Women with Bipolar Disorder: Age and Gender Comparison." *Journal of Psychiatric Research* 43 (8): 798–802.

McKay, M., M. Davis, and P. Fanning. 1997. *Thoughts and Feelings: Taking Control of Your Moods and Your Life.* 2nd ed. Oakland, CA: New Harbinger Publications.

Miklowitz, D. 2010. *The Bipolar Survival Guide: What You and Your Family Need to Know.* 2nd ed. New York: Guilford Press.

Miklowitz, D. J., D. A. Axelson, B. Birmaher, E. L. George, D. O. Taylor, C. D. Schneck, C. A. Beresford, L. M. Dickinson, W. E. Craighead, and D. A. Brent. 2008. "Family-Focused Treatment for Adolescents with Bipolar Disorder: Results of a 2-Year Randomized Trial." *Archives of General Psychiatry* 65 (9): 1053–61.

Miklowitz, D. J., and M. J. Goldstein. 1997. *Bipolar Disorder: A Family-Focused Treatment Approach.* New York: Guilford Press.

Miklowitz, D. J., and B. S. L. Johnson. 2009. "Social and Familial Factors in the Course of Bipolar Disorder: Basic Processes and Relevant Interventions." *Clinical Psychology: Science and Practice* 16 (2): 281–96.

Miklowitz, D. J., M. W. Otto, E. Frank, N. A. Reilly-Harrington, J. N. Kogan, G. S. Sachs, et al. 2007. "Intensive Psychosocial Intervention Enhances Functioning in Patients with Bipolar Depression: Results from a 9-Month Randomized Controlled Trial." *American Journal of Psychiatry* 164 (9): 1340–47.

Miklowitz, D. J., M. W. Otto, E. Frank, N. A. Reilly-Harrington, S. R. Wisniewski, J. N. Kogan, et al. 2007. "Psychosocial Treatments for Bipolar Depression: A 1-Year Randomized Trial from the Systematic Treatment Enhancement Program." *Archives of General Psychiatry* 64 (4): 419–26.

Miklowitz, D. J., T. L. Simoneau, E. L. George, J. A. Richards, A. Kalbag, N. Sachs-Ericsson, and R. Suddath. 2000. "Family-Focused Treatment of Bipolar Disorder: 1-Year Effects of a Psychoeducational Program in Conjunction with Pharmacotherapy." *Biological Psychiatry* 48 (6): 582–92.

Miller, J. J., K. Fletcher, and J. Kabat-Zinn. 1995. "Three-Year Follow-up and Clinical Implications of a Mindfulness Meditation-Based Stress Reduction Intervention in the Treatment of Anxiety Disorders." *General Hospital Psychiatry* 17 (3): 192–200.

Munk-Olsen, T., T. M. Laursen, T. Mendelson, C. B. Pedersen, O. Mors, and P. B. Mortensen. 2009. "Risks and Predictors of Readmission for a Mental Disorder During the Postpartum Period." *Archives of General Psychiatry* 66 (2): 189–95.

Newman, C. F., R. L. Leahy, A. T. Beck, N. A. Reilly-Harrington, and L. Gyulai. 2002. *Bipolar Disorder: A Cognitive Therapy Approach.* Washington, DC: American Psychological Association.

Ng, F., S. Dodd, and M. Berk. 2007. "The Effects of Physical Activity in the Acute Treatment of Bipolar Disorder: A Pilot Study." *Journal of Affective Disorders* 101 (1-3): 259–62.

Nolen-Hoeksema, S., and J. Morrow. 1991. "A Prospective Study of Depression and Posttraumatic Stress Symptoms After a Natural Disaster: The 1989 Loma Prieta Earthquake." *Journal of Personality & Social Psychology* 61 (1): 115–21.

Payne, J. L., P. S. Roy, K. Murphy-Eberenz, M. M. Weismann, K. L. Swartz, M. G. McInnis, et al. 2007. "Reproductive Cycle-Associated Mood Symptoms in Women with Major Depression and Bipolar Disorder." *Journal of Affective Disorders* 99 (1-3): 221–29.

Perich, T., V. Manicavasagar, P. B. Mitchell, J. R. Ball, and D. Hadzi-Pavlovic. 2013. "A Randomized Controlled Trial of Mindfulness-Based Cognitive Therapy for Bipolar Disorder." *Acta Psychiatrica Scandinavica* 127 (5): 333–43.

Perry, A., N. Tarrier, R. Morriss, E. McCarthy, and K. Limb. 1999. "Randomised Controlled Trial of Efficacy of Teaching Patients with Bipolar Disorder to Identify Early Symptoms of Relapse and Obtain Treatment." *British Medical Journal* 318 (7177): 149–53.

Pinheiro, K. A., F. M. Coelho, L. Quevedo, K. Jansen, L. Souza, J. P. Oses, B. L. Horta, R. A. da Silva, and R. T. Pinheiro. 2011. "Paternal Postpartum Mood: Bipolar Episodes?" *Revista Brasileira de Psiquiatria* 33 (3): 283–86.

Quevedo L., R. A. da Silva, F. Coelho, K. A. Pinheiro, B. L. Horta, F. Kapczinski, and R. T. Pinheiro. 2011. "Risk of Suicide and Mixed Episode in Men in the Postpartum Period." *Journal of Affective Disorders* 132 (1-2): 243–46.

Rathus, J. H., and A. L. Miller. 2002. "Dialectical Behavior Therapy Adapted for Suicidal Adolescents." *Suicide and Life-Threatening Behavior* 32 (2): 146–57.

Reilly-Harrington, N. A., L. B. Alloy, D. M. Fresco, and W. G. Whitehouse. 1999. "Cognitive Styles and Life Events Interact to Predict Bipolar and Unipolar Symptomatology." *Journal of Abnormal Psychology* 108 (4): 567–78.

Roosevelt, F. D. 1938. "Franklin D. Roosevelt, Inaugural Address, March 4, 1933." In *The Public Papers of Franklin D. Roosevelt, Volume Two: The Year of Crisis, 1933*, edited by S. Rosenman, 11–16. New York: Random House.

Sachs, G. S., A. A. Nierenberg, J. R. Calabrese, L. B. Marangell, S. R. Wisniewski, L. Gyulai, et al. 2007. "Effectiveness of Adjunctive Antidepressant Treatment for Bipolar Depression." *New England Journal of Medicine* 356 (17): 1711–22.

Sachs, G. S., M. E. Thase, M. W. Otto, M. Bauer, D. Miklowitz, S. R. Wisniewski, et al. 2003. "Rationale, Design, and Methods of the Systematic Treatment Enhancement Program for Bipolar Disorder (STEP-BD)." *Biological Psychiatry* 53 (11): 1028–42.

Safer, D. L., C. F. Telch, and W. S. Agras. 2001. "Dialectical Behavior Therapy for Bulimia Nervosa." *American Journal of Psychiatry* 158 (4): 632–34.

Sapp, M. 1994. "The Effects of Guided Imagery on Reducing the Worry and Emotionality Components of Test Anxiety." *Journal of Mental Imagery* 18(3–4): 165–79.

Scott, J. 2001. "Cognitive Therapy as an Adjunct to Medication in Bipolar Disorder." *British Journal of Psychiatry* 178 (Suppl. 41): S164–68.

Scott, J., E. Paykel, R. Morriss, R. Bentall, P. Kinderman, T. Johnson, R. Abbott, and H. Hayhurst. 2006. "Cognitive-Behavioural Therapy for Severe and Recurrent Bipolar Disorders: Randomised Controlled Trial." *British Journal of Psychiatry* 188(4): 313–20.

Segal, Z. V., J. M. G. Williams, and J. D. Teasdale. 2002. *Mindfulness-Based Cognitive Therapy for Depression: A New Approach to Preventing Relapse.* New York: Guilford Press.

Serretti, A., L. Mandelli, E. Lattuada, C. Cusin, and E. Smeraldi. 2002. "Clinical and Demographic Features of Mood Disorder Subtypes." *Psychiatry Research* 112 (3): 195–210.

Shen, G. H., L. B. Alloy, L. Y. Abramson, and L. G. Sylvia. 2008. "Social Rhythm Regularity and the Onset of Affective Episodes in Bipolar Spectrum Individuals." *Bipolar Disorders* 10 (4): 520–29.

Simon, N. M., M. W. Otto, S. R. Wisniewski, M. Fossey, K. Sagduyu, E. Frank, G. S. Sachs, A. A. Nierenberg, M. E. Thase, and M. H. Pollack. 2004. "Anxiety Disorder Comorbidity in Bipolar Disorder Patients: Data from the First 500 Participants in the Systematic Treatment Enhancement Program for Bipolar Disorder (STEP-BD)." *American Journal of Psychiatry* 161 (12): 2222–29.

Soreca, I., E. Frank, and D. J. Kupfer. 2009. "The Phenomenology of Bipolar Disorder: What Drives the High Rate of Medical Burden and Determines Long-Term Prognosis?" *Depression and Anxiety* 26 (1): 73–82.

Stathopoulou, G., M. B. Powers, A. C. Berry, J. A. J. Smits, and M. W. Otto. 2006. "Exercise Interventions for Mental Health: A Quantitative and Qualitative Review." *Clinical Psychology: Science and Practice* 13 (2): 179–93.

Sylvia, L. G., A. A. Nierenberg, J. P. Stange, A. D. Peckham, and T. Deckersbach. 2011. "Development of an Integrated Psychosocial Treatment to Address the Medical Burden Associated with Bipolar Disorder." *Journal of Psychiatric Practice* 17 (3): 224–32.

Teasdale, J. D., Z. V. Segal, J. M. Williams, V. A. Ridgeway, J. M. Soulsby, and M. A. Lau. 2000. "Prevention of Relapse/Recurrence in Major Depression by Mindfulness-Based Cognitive Therapy." *Journal of Consulting and Clinical Psychology* 68 (4): 615–23.

Telch, C. F., W. S. Agras, and M. M. Linehan. 2001. "Dialectical Behavior Therapy for Binge Eating Disorder." *Journal of Consulting and Clinical Psychology* 69 (6): 1061–65.

Van Dijk, S. 2009. *The Dialectical Behavior Therapy Skills Workbook for Bipolar Disorder.* Oakland, CA: New Harbinger Publications.

Verheul, R., L. M. van den Bosch, M. W. Koeter, M. A. de Ridder, T. Stijnen, and W. van den Brink. 2003. "Dialectical Behaviour Therapy for Women with Borderline Personality Disorder: 12-Month, Randomised Clinical Trial in The Netherlands." *British Journal of Psychiatry* 182(2): 135–40.

Wegner, D. M. 1994. *White Bears and Other Unwanted Thoughts: Suppression, Obsession, and the Psychology of Mental Control.* New York: Guilford Press.

Wegner, D. M., D. J. Schneider, S. Carter, and T. L. White. 1987. "Paradoxical Effects of Thought Suppression." *Journal of Personality and Social Psychology* 53(1): 5–13.

Wehr, T. A., D. A. Sack, and N. E. Rosenthal. 1987. "Sleep Reduction as a Final Common Pathway in the Genesis of Mania." *American Journal of Psychiatry* 144 (2): 201–4.

Williams, M., J. D. Teasdale, Z. V. Segal, and J. Kabat-Zinn. 2007. *The Mindful Way Through Depression: Freeing Yourself from Chronic Unhappiness*. New York: Guilford Press.

Wurtzel, E. 1994. *Prozac Nation: Young and Depressed in America*. Boston: Houghton Mifflin.

Yan, L. J., C. Hammen, A. N. Cohen, S. E. Daley, and R. M. Henry. 2004. "Expressed Emotion Versus Relationship Quality Variables in the Prediction of Recurrence in Bipolar Patients." *Journal of Affective Disorders* 83 (2-3): 199–206.

Zaretsky, A. E., Z. V. Segal, and M. Gemar. 1999. "Cognitive Therapy for Bipolar Depression: A Pilot Study." *Canadian Journal of Psychiatry* 44 (5): 491–94.

Stephanie McMurrich Roberts, PhD, is a clinical psychologist specializing in the cognitive-behavioral treatment of mood and anxiety disorders. Roberts has published a number of peer-reviewed articles related to bipolar disorder and depression. A former instructor in psychology at Harvard Medical School and staff psychologist at the Massachusetts General Hospital Bipolar Clinic and Research Program, she now works in private practice in Boston, MA.

Louisa Grandin Sylvia, PhD, is associate director of psychology at the Massachusetts General Hospital Bipolar Clinic and Research Program and assistant professor at Harvard Medical School. Sylvia is a skilled cognitive-behavioral therapist who develops psychosocial interventions for bipolar disorder. She is currently examining the efficacy of nutrition, exercise, and wellness therapy for bipolar disorder. Sylvia has presented her work at local, national, and international conferences, and has authored many empirically-based articles on the treatment and prevention of bipolar episodes.

Noreen A. Reilly-Harrington, PhD, is an internationally recognized expert on the cognitive-behavioral treatment of bipolar disorder and has coauthored several books and numerous scientific articles on bipolar disorder. For the past seventeen years, she has been on the staff of the Massachusetts General Hospital Bipolar Clinic and Research Program and on the faculty of Harvard Medical School. She has trained thousands of clinicians for academic and industry-sponsored studies in the assessment, diagnosis, and treatment of bipolar disorder, and currently serves as the director of training and assessment for the Bipolar Trials Network.

Foreword writer **David J. Miklowitz, PhD**, is professor of psychiatry in the division of child and adolescent psychiatry at the University of California, Los Angeles's Semel Institute; a senior research fellow in the department of psychiatry at Oxford University; and the author of several articles and books on bipolar disorder and schizophrenia, including *The Bipolar Disorder Survival Guide*, an international best seller.

FROM OUR PUBLISHER—

As the publisher at New Harbinger and a clinical psychologist since 1978, I know that emotional problems are best helped with evidence-based therapies. These are the treatments derived from scientific research (randomized controlled trials) that show what works. Whether these treatments are delivered by trained clinicians or found in a self-help book, they are designed to provide you with proven strategies to overcome your problem.

Therapies that aren't evidence-based—whether offered by clinicians or in books—are much less likely to help. In fact, therapies that aren't guided by science may not help you at all. That's why this New Harbinger book is based on scientific evidence that the treatment can relieve emotional pain.

This is important: if this book isn't enough, and you need the help of a skilled therapist, use the following resources to find a clinician trained in the evidence-based protocols appropriate for your problem. And if you need more support—a community that understands what you're going through and can show you ways to cope—resources for that are provided below, as well.

Real help is available for the problems you have been struggling with. The skills you can learn from evidence-based therapies will change your life.

Matthew McKay, PhD
Publisher, New Harbinger Publications

If you need a therapist, the following organization can help you find a therapist trained in cognitive behavioral therapy (CBT).

The Association for Behavioral & Cognitive Therapies (ABCT) Find-a-Therapist service offers a list of therapists schooled in CBT techniques. Therapists listed are licensed professionals who have met the membership requirements of ABCT and who have chosen to appear in the directory.

Please visit www.abct.org and click on *Find a Therapist*.

For additional support for patients, family, and friends, please contact the following:

Depression and Bipolar Support Alliance (DBSA) **Visit www.dbsalliance.org**

National Alliance on Mental Illness (NAMI) **Visit www.nami.org**

Bipolar Happens **Visit www.bipolarhappens.com**

National Suicide Prevention Lifeline
Call 24 hours a day 1-800-273-TALK (8255) or visit suicidepreventionlifeline.org

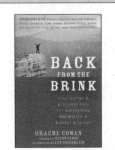

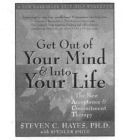

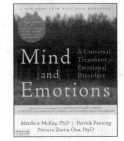
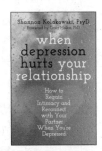

Real change *is* possible

For more than forty-five years, New Harbinger has published proven-effective self-help books and pioneering workbooks to help readers of all ages and backgrounds improve mental health and well-being, and achieve lasting personal growth. In addition, our spirituality books offer profound guidance for deepening awareness and cultivating healing, self-discovery, and fulfillment.

Founded by psychologist Matthew McKay and Patrick Fanning, New Harbinger is proud to be an independent, employee-owned company. Our books reflect our core values of integrity, innovation, commitment, sustainability, compassion, and trust. Written by leaders in the field and recommended by therapists worldwide, New Harbinger books are practical, accessible, and provide real tools for real change.

newharbingerpublications